T0065379

I CHOOSE TO WIN

PERRY L WALKER JR.

WESTBOW
PRESS®
A DIVISION OF THOMAS NELSON
& ZONDERVAN

WestBow Press books may be ordered through booksellers or by contacting:

WestBow Press
A Division of Thomas Nelson & Zondervan
1663 Liberty Drive
Bloomington, IN 47403
www.westbowpress.com
1 (866) 928-1240

ISBN: 978-1-6642-0069-2 (sc)
ISBN: 978-1-6642-0070-8 (e)

Print information available on the last page.

WestBow Press rev. date: 08/22/2020

CONTENTS

DEDICATION

I would like to dedicate this book to all of you who are persistent in following your dreams, even in the face of extreme adversity. I do understand that some of you may not share my religious views. This book is not intended to push my beliefs, but rather to let you know that there is someone who has been in your shoes.

My faith in God is what drives me. While I still have breath in my lungs, the joy I have in Christ keeps me focused on fulfilling my God-given purpose. It is my desire that everyone reading this book would get to know Jesus as their Lord and Savior. Anyhow, this one is for you. I am not your judge, I am your friend, and I pray that this book brings you encouragement as you push towards fulfilling your purpose in life.

ACKNOWLEDGMENTS

First, I would like to thank my Lord and Savior, Jesus Christ, for saving me and giving me the courage to share such intimate details of my life in this book. Christ has been my strength, and indeed my reason for being. Next, I would like to thank my beautiful wife of twenty-four years for always being there for me. Even during the times when I was not pleasant to be around, we have never cursed, physically abused, or been unfaithful to one another. When most women would have thrown in the towel, she stayed right here, always encouraging, respecting, and loving me.

I would like to thank my mother for working hard and doing the best she could for my siblings and me. I would like to thank my children and the rest of my family for being so awesome. I would also like to thank "Mommy," Beverly Wilson. Thank you for your prayers, wisdom, and Godly advice.

The next group of people I would like to thank is Pastor Jody and Kathy Nichols. You guys were indeed used by God to help mend my marriage when I was a young and foolish man. The time we spent at Open Arms Fellowship as members were some of the most cherished times in our lives. Thank you for being a Godly inspiration to my family. To Randy and Pam Nichols, thank you for making my family a part of your family while we were at Open Arms Fellowship. We really enjoyed the times we spent together hanging out on Sunday afternoons. Thank you, Ray and Mom Sue Christian, for adopting my family and me as your family while we were living in Minnesota so far away from home. You all are our family, and I appreciate you. I would also like to thank Ben & Ruth Lee, Mark & Karen Warner, The Myerson family, Bob & Mary Bayer, and Pastor Gordy & family. All of you were our family.

You made Minnesota a "home away from home." You were a source of strength, and I will never forget your kindness. I would also like to thank Toussant and Jacqueline Smith for being such great friends and blessings in our lives. I would further like to thank Mom Merine and her family for being such a tremendous blessing. To my surrogate mother, Sharon Boyd, thanks for believing in me.

Last but not least, I would like to thank Reverend and Pastor Flowers for being such remarkable leaders for my family.

FOREWORD

Hello, let me introduce myself. My name is Keshah Darden Walker. I am the wife of this amazing man, Perry Walker, the author, and writer of this book. I have lived through every episode written within these pages for the last 24 years. I have experienced the highs and the lows with Perry. I have also witnessed the awesome power of God with this man; I look forward to many more.

This book is not a how-to book. This book is a book about choosing to win whether life is going your way or not and how we navigate the twist and turns during the journey. How we handle choices, we make whether good or bad. This book will tell you about my husband and his battle with low self-esteem. How having low self-esteem and not really, or let me say, not knowing how to depend on God almost destroyed our family. However, God is faithful, and my husband had a desire to win, so he chose to win. He asked God for help, and God gave my husband the strength and courage to fight.

During this read, I promise you will cry, and I promise you will laugh at some of the things Perry and I went through. As we went over the book, I remembered what we went through. We also laughed and cried. God is faithful because, on September 8, 1996, I married a man who did not know who he was. Fast forward 24 years later. I'm married to a man who knows who he is and who's he is. He is a man of God! He is my King! He is a man who **"Chooses to Win!"**

I love you, babe.
Keshah Darden Walker

ONE
IDENTITY CRISIS

Have you ever pretended to be someone else or someone you admired? I know I have. When the movie "Rocky" first came out, my family went to see it at the State Theater in downtown Austin. Back then, the theaters only had one or two screens. When a big movie featured, it was difficult to see that movie on the opening night. You had to get to the theater early. If not, you had to settle for watching a different film until you could see the one you wanted to see on another day. I remember being captivated by Rocky's bravery, strength, and determination, not to quit. After the movie was over, I recall walking out of the theater, feeling like I was Rocky. I imagined that everyone was looking at me, admiring the strength and bravery that was exuding from my being.

Everything I admired about the character Rocky, I wanted to be, at least until I found another object of admiration. I was seven then, and like most children, I changed heroes like a mother changes a baby's diaper, which is often. Even as a teen, I not only admired fictitious characters but also some of my peers. I especially admired those who embodied the qualities I did not possess but wanted so desperately to have. I understand that it is perfectly normal to have heroes when you are young. I believe that having heroes and mentors to model your life after when you are an adult is excellent as well. I have had many mentors in my life. Some people did not know that they were mentoring me, and some people did. It is an honorable thing to be a mentor, and the right type of mentorship can boost one's quality of life. However, there was a time when my admiration for those whom I saw as heroes were unhealthy. I did not like who I was, and my self-esteem was very low. As a young boy, I felt I had no direction, and this carried over into most of my adult life. What I was suffering from was an identity crisis. In this present time, I believe there are a lot of people today who are suffering from an identity crisis. It does not matter if you are poor, wealthy, unemployed, or at the top of the corporate ladder; you could still be suffering from an identity crisis. My crisis started when I was very young before I even understood or could also say the word 'crisis.' I would like to explain how it began.

I am the youngest of three children born from my mother's first marriage. My mother and my biological father divorced when I was around two-years-old, and she remarried when I was about four. I do not have many early memories of my biological father before the age of five. I do remember images of a black man, a Christmas tree in an apartment, passing a pearl beer sign while riding in a car, and the smell of cigarette smoke. I also remember his voice. It wasn't until I was five when I became aware of whom my biological father was. Before that, I thought my stepfather was my real father. I really did not know when my stepdad came into my life, but it felt like he was always there. My birth father's presence in my life was more of a cameo, a few appearances here and there. He left as quickly as he arrived. It is strange, but as children, my siblings and I were excited to see him when he came to see us. Unfortunately, our excitement would often turn into disappointment. He would sometimes not show up or call to explain why he did not visit us.

I can recall several times when my siblings and I waited from dawn until dusk for him. He called and said he was coming to town to see us. When it started to get dark, my older brother would tell us, "Daddy's not coming." My older sister would get upset, but I did not give up hope. I'd run to the window whenever I heard what sounded like a car pulling into the driveway or see what appeared to be a car's headlights. But no matter how many times he'd disappoint us when he did show up, we were excited to see him. He was our hero. As young children, all that mattered was that we got to see our daddy. My stepfather and my biological father did not get along. I never understood why until I was much older. As a child, all I saw and heard when those two interacted was flaring tempers, fussing, and a lot of cussing. My stepfather was a deeply hurt man. He was a heavy drinker and was often drunk. There is hardly a time I can remember him being sober. Naturally, as a child and being the youngest before my little brother was born, I tried to look up to him as a father figure, hero, and mentor.

I once called him "Dad' when I was seven or eight. He promptly corrected me by saying, "Your Dad lives in Houston." I don't believe he deliberately tried to disown or reject me, but as a child, the comment made me feel that way. On one side of the coin, I had a father who was not making an effort to be involved in my life and gave a lot of excuses for why he couldn't. On the other side, the only male figure I could physically see daily did not provide much interaction except for disciplinary action. I felt I had no identity, and no one I could look up too. I believe that is why it was so hard for me to see God as my Father when I first became a Christian. My home life was not the standard for healthy relationships by no stretch of the imagination. I know my upbringing is synonymous with millions of people from all walks of life and around the world. In fact, there are others whose upbringing was so bad it would make Oliver Twist look like a crown prince. However, I do believe how someone is raised, and their home training can set the stage for failure or success. I believe success does not equate to financial gain or elevated social status. The Bible says to:

> Train up a child the way he should go and when he is old
> he will not depart from it. Proverbs 22:6 (NKJV)

This scripture is a powerful statement. As a parent, it is our responsibility to train our children and point them in the right direction. The scripture also says:

> Like arrows in the hand of a warrior, so are the children
> of one's youth. Psalm 127:4 (NKJV)

By no means am I advocating blaming one's childhood for the way life has turned out. However, there is a standard of parenting that must live in the home. This standard is the only way for a child to reach their maximum potential. Without Godly parenting, it is impossible to give a child their best start. Unfortunately, many people were not provided a good foundation.

> *Unless the Lord builds the house, they labor in vain who build it; unless the Lord guards the city, the watchman stays awake in vain. Psalms 127:1 (NKJV)*

As I mentioned, my biological father stopped by our house every once in a while. He even sent money so that my siblings and I could buy school clothes. He imparted nothing to help me develop as a young man, point me to God, or help me find the way. My stepdad worked a job, paid the bills, etc., but again, he gave no wisdom in my growth into manhood. I did not know where to find my identity. I am not bashing my real father or my stepdad; neither of them is alive today. I love them both and came to forgive them. I asked God to forgive me for being angry with them for so many years.

However, I must be truthful. My intentions are not to offend or present a negative image of my father or my stepdad. I am just emphasizing that it is imperative that children have a sense of direction and identity that is passed on to them by their fathers. In the book "Where Are the Men?", Pastor Jacqueline Flowers says: "The behavior of the man is vitally important to the behavior of the children and spouse."[1] I certainly believe this to be true.

As a young boy, I had a fear of my stepdad when he was drunk. I often felt useless, helpless, and afraid. Because of this, I lacked the spirit of competitiveness and would concede to cowardice behavior when challenged by other males my age. I would naturally believe that I could not win whatever contest that was presented, play any sport well, make good grades, etc. The funny thing is that I attracted other children with the same behavior. We were neither leaders nor followers; we did not even fit in with the children that referred to as nerds. It was like we had no real place. Our family structures were also similar in many ways. Whether it was alcoholism or drug abuse, we were all a part of a blended family produced by divorce. My greatest fear of growing up

---

[1] Pastor Jacqueline T Flowers, *Where are the Men*, 1st ed. (Tamarac, FL: Llumina Christian Books, 2011), 19.

was that I would end up like my stepdad or my father when I became a man. Would I be an abusive husband that will walk out on my wife and children for other women? Would I be a violent drunk that would verbally and physically abuse my family? Oh, God was I was terrified of this. Can you imagine being an adolescent harboring these types of thoughts and feelings?

Along with the fear of failure and low esteem, these tormenting thoughts played a vital role in how my teenage and most of my adult life turned out. The statement "sticks and stones will break my bones, but words will never hurt me" **is a lie**. Words do hurt. There are plenty of us who are destroying ourselves with the words we say to ourselves, compounded with the hurtful words said to us by others. Parents, we must watch what we say to our children and listen to what our children are saying to themselves. Speak the Word of God over them, and they must see you speak the Word of God over your life and believing it. Success in life is not dressed up in lofty titles and money, but rather by the words we speak. Children must be taught how to speak life and to start speaking life early. I did not know how to speak words of life, and I did not hear "life words" spoken in my household. If parents would train their children, they will know the way to go and strive to stay on course. They will learn their identity and know who they are and that they are unique. Our children belong to God. Think about it, why do people say, "I need to find myself?" It is because they were not shown or taught who they are.

Let me clarify this for us, so-called Christian parents. Going to church, saying grace before you eat, or even reading the Bible at bedtime to your children is not all it takes to train the child. All of those things are great and beneficial. Still, if they are done out of tradition rather than a committed relationship with Jesus Christ, it is all for naught. We must walk out our salvation before our children, modeling Christ-like behavior, and apply God's Word to our lives daily. This will give security to our children because they will see your faithfulness and that you know who you are in Christ. They will follow in your footsteps and embrace the uniqueness God has given them to be everything He has created them to be.

Many times a child or adolescent's behavior is viewed as rebellious when, in essence, they are just reflecting what they have been exposed to or the lack of proper parental training. I am not a psychologist, and by no means am I qualified to give medical advice. However, when we look at the degradation of our youth in America, it does not take a doctor to explain the obvious. As a parent, I have been guilty of sending mixed messages to my children. I have seen many of the issues I've struggled with my entire life, which my children have never seen, manifested in their behavior. In the past, some scientists believed that a person's basic character traits can be inherited from their parents through their genes. Some scientists also thought that the behavior and a person's moral character are determined by the environment he is raised in. I am no expert in the behavioral sciences and certainly don't have any authority to expound on the subject. However, I believe King David referred to this similar issue when he repented from committing adultery with Bathsheba and having her husband Uriah killed. He said:

> *Behold, I was brought forth in iniquity, And in sin my mother conceived me.: Psalm 51:5 (NKJV)*

I believe David is expressing that he was born within a sinful world, with a sinful nature with the propensity to do evil and that he needed God to cleanse him. This is why I feel that it is essential that parents model Christ before their children and foster a holy environment in their homes. We can combat harmful behavioral patterns that are past down from previous generations through the power of Christ. Paul writes in the book of Romans:

> *Therefore, just as through one man sin entered the world, and death through sin, and thus death spread to all men, because all sinned—. Romans 5:12 (NKJV)*

Because of Adam's fall, man's nature is bent towards sin. The unpredictability of that nature spawns a plethora of behavioral issues that can only be healed by the nurturing of God's word. Still, our sinful nature does not give me or anyone else an excuse to say, "I was born this way." We do have a choice to rise above the sinful nature we were born with, through Christ. Today, I no longer suffer from an identity crisis. As a father of four beautiful children, I am doing my best to ensure that they have a solid foundation. I made a lot of mistakes, but I am pressing forward. The problem with facing an identity crisis is that you tend to feel trapped and drift through life with no sense of real purpose. I liken it to what the Apostle Paul says:

> *That we henceforth be no more children, tossed to and fro, and carried about with every wind of doctrine, by the sleight of men, and cunning craftiness, whereby they lie in wait to deceive. Ephesians 4:14 (KJV)*

This verse is referring to matters of doctrinal truth. I believe that if one is not sure of whom they are, they will fall for anything. This state of mind is susceptible to being led astray towards empty promises, envy for another person's life or possessions, and even being driven to harming one's self. There was a time in my life when I thought it would be better for my wife and children if I were dead and tried to commit suicide. I thought that my death would allow them to receive better benefits from the state of Texas that would take care of their needs. How selfish and misguided was my thinking! I put my family in harm's way and opened a door for Satan to wreak havoc in their lives. An identity crisis will cloud judgment, produce selfish behavior, jealousy, envy, instability, and "tosses you to and fro" through the waves of life.

It is not hard to notice someone suffering through an identity crisis. There are visible signs such as an outward display of low self-esteem, controlling personality, addictions of all sorts, people-pleasing, and a tendency to mimic or star gaze (thinking more highly of people than you should). Some suffer from an identity crisis that is either overly confident or has the false appearance of being humble and modest. Both types can give the impression of someone being strong and assertive with a sense of direction or the latter, being generous or selfless. If investigated closer, you may find this may not be the case. Just within the last two decades alone, we have seen several famous people die prematurely from self-inflicted harm. Some were obviously confused about who they were, and others came as a complete surprise, at least to those who did not know them intimately. Now, think about the numerous people who are not famous who have died prematurely; those who are living and struggling with the same thing. Let me be clear about something; when I refer to an identity crisis, I am not making references to gender confusion or alternate lifestyles. I am a Christian, and I firmly believe that anyone struggling with gender or alternative lifestyle issues is obviously having an identity crisis. The only help for that is Christ. Consequently, the only relief for **all** identity issues is in Jesus Christ.

> *For in Him we live and move, and have our being; as certain also of your own poets have said, for we are His offspring. Acts 17.28 (KJV).*

Amid my own identity struggles before, and after I became a Christian, I tried counseling from a psychologist and psychiatrist who put me on medication, but none of that helped me. It wasn't until I truly made a decision to trust God wholeheartedly that I saw a breakthrough. I began my journey towards winning in life. I respect those who choose that profession and continuously help people. I am not belittling the need we have for them in our society. There are a lot of excellent counselors to choose from. However, I believe that God is infinite in wisdom and that without Him, there is no chance of recovery from a confused identity of any sort. At least for me, I can say Christ made the difference. I no longer see myself as inferior, nor do I cower at a challenge. Circumspectly, I am facing some tough challenges even as I write this book. And so is the rest of the world with the advent of COVID-19. Winning in life is not just about arriving at some apex or achieving first place in a contest, it is a daily event. Winning is a choice, and I faced many hardships until I realized it.

Some of you who are reading this book may be facing impossible odds, fears, or have a similar background as I do. Some of you may feel ashamed because you profess to be a Christian, but yet you are struggling to see yourself the way God sees you. I drove my wife bananas for the first ten years of our marriage. I was very negative, and I spoke a lot of "death talk" and doubt. I put my family through so much pain. An identity crisis can affect everyone around you. It repels, consumes, and overtakes everything we hold dear or precious. My children started taking on the character I modeled before them. I tried to be very careful and not speak "doom and gloom" around them, but that did not matter. I spoke it into the atmosphere, into existence, whether they heard it or not, and it permeated through my home. The bible says,

Life and death are in the power of the tongue, and those who love it will eat its fruit. Proverbs 18:21 (HCSB)

I was eating the fruit of what I was speaking and could not understand why my family and I were experiencing so many hardships. My foundation was set. I earlier explained the relationship I had with my fathers. However, I still had a choice to make. I was angry with them, envious of other people's progress in life, and even bitter with my wife. My friend, you may be at a crossroads in your life. You may feel you are stuck on a vicious roller coaster and not sure of who you are or where you are going. You may even be a CEO at the height of your career, trying to keep up the image of success, but you feel empty inside like the life you are living is for someone else. Like my wife said in the foreword, this is not a how-to book. I can't give you advice about the next stock market boom or show you how to amass great material wealth. What I do have to offer, I give to you freely. It is your choice. The choice is free, but the cost is high. Too many times, we look for a magical cure to heal our lives without applying a real effort to change. There are a lot of good self-help books out in the market today written by some of the sharpest minds of the 20th and 21st centuries. Still, none of them will do any good if they are simply viewed as a miracle cure to a disease. In the next few chapters, I would like to share with you more of my life and how I decided I will win and the many phases I went through before I made this choice.

TWO

THE WANDERER

Before graduating from high school, I was inwardly terrified with the possibility of facing the world because I had no idea what I was going to do with my life. My grades were not good enough for college, and I was still battling with who I was as a person. Without any thought to the matter, I decided to join the Marines. I figured that if there was any organization on the planet that would help me gain confidence and direction, the U.S Marines was it. Needless to say, my boot camp experience turned out to be very interesting. I did not realize that there were so many colorful adjectives to describe one's lowly existence on the earth. I knew that the Marines were the toughest branch in the military. Still, for some reason, I had it in my mind that the people I meet would become this instant band of brothers, but this was not the case. In boot camp, I faced the same inward challenges I did before joining the Marines. I was a part of a squad with several people, all with different personalities. Some of the guys had dominating personalities; some were self-absorbed, fearful, while others were friendly. The self-proclaimed tough guys went around bossing the other recruits as they were competing for the guide or squad leader positions. Naturally, I stayed out of the race and did my own thing. However, I ended up becoming the Guide, which was a position over the four squad leaders and the platoon. I did not want to show my lack of resolve to these guys, but I hated every minute of being responsible for someone else. I was often challenged by some of the other recruits who saw themselves as the better choice for the guide position. I do not know how I earned their respect, but I had the best fitness and knowledge scores in my platoon.

Nonetheless, I ended up losing the Guide position close to graduation and was demoted to the 4th squad leader position. I believe I had lost the job due to my confidence issues. Even though I managed to get the squad leader position, I never had the full assurance or self-affirmation of being a confident leader. Thankfully, I somehow managed to make it through boot camp and into the fleet. My first duty station was Okinawa, Japan, and like most young men that were far away from the reach of their parents, I got involved with the nightlife quickly. I did everything from buying prostitutes and heavy drinking; you name it, I did it. One would think that being a Marine, I would have had more discipline, but living this life appeared to win me friends and a false sense of self-worth.

I was lost and was enjoying the pleasure of sin. Even then, God had mercy on me because I had many encounters with Christians that would try to minister to me. I recall one of those incidents on a Friday night when I was at the Kadena Air Force base, on my way to have a good time. I was stopped by a Christian, and he proceeded to tell me about Jesus. He read the parable of the sower. When he was finished, he asked me which seed was I, and for some reason, I could not lie. I told him I was the seed that fell among the thorns that were too concerned about the cares of this world. This encounter rattled me to the point where I walked away, wondering about the direction of my life. I would like to say that this encounter brought about a change in my lifestyle choices. Still, unfortunately, soon after, I continued on my night of bar hopping. However, I continued to think about that night and attempted to find religion by attending church. The first church I visited was a charismatic church that a friend of mine attended and invited me to. When we arrived at the church, I thought I had stepped into the twilight zone; everyone was moaning, jumping up and down, and babbling in a weird chant, which now I know to be speaking in tongues. This is pretty much how the whole service went, all three hours of it. There was no preaching or teaching, just repetitious chanting and an occasional song coupled with lots of moaning and crying. Needless to say, I did not visit that church again. After having such a colorful experience at my friend's church, I decided to attend church at the base chapel the following Sunday. Unlike the other church, the base chapel was on the other end of the spectrum, incredibly dull and lifeless. In *lieu* of my experiences with both of those churches, I concluded that pursuing religion was not for me. Notice I did not say pursuing a relationship with God but pursuing religion. I believe there is a difference, and at that time in my life, I did not understand that. First of all, God pursues **us** first, but our sinful nature does not want God. The scripture says:

> *There is no one who understands, there is no one who seeks God. Romans 3:11 (HCSB)*

God was in hot pursuit of me on Okinawa; however, I was not privy to understanding what it meant to have a relationship with God. I pursued Him more as an ideal and philosophy. So as the parable says, the cares and worries of this world choked the Word right out of me.

Because I could not find satisfaction from religion, I sought it more in sex and drinking. I became a wanderer, aimlessly drifting from one mess to another being senseless and foolish. Webster Dictionary defines a "wanderer" as 1. to move about without a definite destination or purpose. 2. To go by an indirect route or at no set pace; amble. 3. To proceed in an irregular course, meander. 4. To behave in a manner that does not conform to morality or norms: wander from the path of righteousness. 5. To turn the attention from one subject to another with little clarity or coherence of thought.[2] The definition described my life to the letter. Another thing about wanderers is that they usually bring chaos to stable environments. For example, if a complainer joins a group of optimistic individuals, it will not be long before the rest of the group starts complaining about something. Isn't it peculiar that a little bit of contamination could be deadly? The bible says it like this:

> *A little yeast leavens the whole lump of dough. Galatians 5:9 (HCSB)*

Whatever the vice of the wandering soul, it will not be long before you see it produce after its own kind. So naturally, I gravitated towards other individuals who were wanderers, and collectively we moved

---

[2] www.merriam-webster.com

nowhere fast. I resented those who were prospering and picked up a rank (got promoted) more quickly than I did. I pretty much gave excuses for my mediocrity. Deep down, I wanted to do well and be respected by my peers, but because I lacked courage and inner strength, I was living my life with the fear of failure. I did not know it at that time, but the bible says:

> For as he thinketh in his heart, so is he: Eat and drink, saith he to thee but his heart is not with thee. *Proverbs 23:7 (KJV)*

Basically, how you see yourself or what you believe about yourself is what you will become. I believe this to be true. All things being equal, if one would take inventory of their thoughts, you will find that your life is a direct reflection of them. If your thoughts are centered on failure, you get failure. If you think success, eventually, you will be successful. I am not merely adopting positive confessions. Confessions are great, but you can say one thing but believe something else in your heart. Notice that the verse from Proverbs says, "as a man thinks in his heart." "Heart" in this passage is synonymous with one's deepest inner being, the core of their thoughts, appetites, and desires. That's why the bible instructs us to take control of our own thoughts:

> Finally, brethren, whatsoever things are true, whatsoever things are honest, whatsoever things are just, whatsoever things are pure, whatsoever things are lovely, whatsoever things are of good report; if there be any virtue, and if there be any praise, think on these things. *Philippians 4:8 (KJV)*

One cannot think per the passage from Philippians if the mind is not renewed from the Word of God. However, the only way the mind can be renewed by the Word of God is if you surrender your life to Jesus Christ. My problem was I did not know Jesus. I was blind to this fact and started resenting the idea and the existence of God. I participated in more rebellious living and did not care who I offended. It seemed like the more I acted this way, the more friends I gained, and the more women were attracted to me. I figured as long as I did unto others what

I wanted them to do unto me, I was being a good person. I spent the first part of my adult life wandering aimlessly like a blind man who, at any time, could have fallen into a deep ditch. I thank God that He had mercy on me and did not let me die in my sins before I even had a chance to truly live.

As I said earlier in the chapter, it appeared that every time I was getting ready to have a night out on the town, I would get stopped by a Christian who would try to tell me about Jesus. I remember I thought in my mind that if I try a different location to get money out of an ATM, I could avoid these Christians; this did not work. It was like they were all over the place, and I would somehow end up getting stopped. Well, I got tired of getting stopped and getting bummed out when confronted with the truth. I did everything I could to avoid them. I got pretty good at spotting them. So good, that for the last 6 months I was in Okinawa, I managed to have undisturbed partying without getting stopped.

Soon, I got stationed in California at Camp Pendleton near Oceanside and San Diego. I was living the dream. I was living the life that my best friend and I dreamed of living when we were children. I had access to all the treats California had to offer, and then it happened; I met a Marine in my unit that was a Christian. He went through his whole, "Do you know Jesus?" solicitation, and I became furious. I did not argue with him at the time. However, he felt the tension. As I walked away, I said in my heart, "If another Christian comes up to me, I am going to bash his head in." One thing I have come to learn about God is that He wins every challenge or battle and do not dare Him. About six months went by, and then in August of 1990, a crazed dictator named Saddam Hussein from Iraq invaded a country called Kuwait. My unit was the first to respond to this threat. The news was portraying this to be the beginning of Armageddon. My buddies and I were very afraid because when we joined the military, fighting in a war was the furthest thing from our mind. Once again, I found myself faced with some hard questions; is there a heaven and hell? Which one would I go to if I were killed in action? You see, one thing about a wandering mind is that there is no certainty. I was not sure about anything, especially then when I was about to be dropped in a war zone where danger is imminent, and death was highly probable. I made another weak attempt to try and tap into religion, but I found no comfort or peace. Not because God was not real, but because I did not know Him. However, as we mobilized further inland from the Mediterranean, I was assigned to a communication group that was not quite on the front lines. This incident caused my fears to fade. With a new sense of comfort and relief, my attempt to "find" religion also faded. Remember earlier that I said that it is not wise to dare God? Well, being over in the Gulf, Christians sprang up like dandelions, and I did my best to avoid them and the scary "end of the world" rhetoric they were preaching. But one day, I let my guard down. I was assigned guard duty. My job duty was to do a bomb search on vehicles that came into our camp. There was a new Corporal of Guard assigned over us; his name was Corporal Green. Now, one thing about Corporal Green is that he looked like the typical tough Marine. He had broad shoulders, a wide neck, and man did he look intimidating. Even with the gruff persona, there was something different about Corporal Green, but I could not put my finger on it. So one day, I got the courage to strike up a conversation with him to try to figure him out. I decided to talk about rap music and my passion for music production. Before I knew it, we were having a great conversation about music and family, and then it happened. He started telling me about how his life has changed since he met Christ, and he has been a Christian for some years. I thought to myself, "I knew something was different about this guy, and now he is going to ask me if I knew Jesus." Guess what? I was right. He asked me if I knew Jesus, and right then, like a flashback, I remembered what I said I would do to the next Christian that would ask me that question. Now, I don't know if God took me seriously, or if He was just showing that He had a sense of humor. Either way, He got my attention. Corporal Green was an enormous man. He was the prime example of what an ideal Marine looks like. God had gotten my attention because He cared enough to meet me where I was, and I guess He did show that He had a sense of humor. Deep down, I was longing for something different, and when my experiment with religion failed, I became angry with God. I thought I had messed up so much that He did not want to know me, kind of like I felt about my biological father. Jesus says:

Come to Me, all of you who are weary and burdened, and I will give you rest. All of you, take up My yoke and learn from Me, because I am gentle and humble in heart, and you will find rest for yourselves. Matthew 11:28-29 (HCSB)

This verse definitely described me and what I desperately needed. Even while I was out in the clubs, I felt no satisfaction, and I knew I was going nowhere fast and could not keep going like I was. Some of you reading this book can identify with me. We know when we are not doing right; even Stevie Wonder could see that, and the last thing we want to hear is something we already know. Eventually, I ended up going back to Corporal Green's barracks to discuss my life and what Jesus did for mankind at the cross. That night, I was tired of running. I was tired of stumbling aimlessly through life with no purpose or direction. I was all out of excuses, and I wanted more. On the night of September 2, 1990, I gave my life to Jesus. I did not see angels descending or hear harps playing, but I knew something was different, and my life would not be the same from that point on.

The next day I told my buddies what I had done, and I did not get the response I wanted. Call me naïve, but I thought my friends would immediately see the change in my life and would ask to be saved as well. After all, I had been a Christian for over twelve hours by then. What I learned that day was that not everyone is going to applaud your decision to follow Christ, and the worst scrutiny you will face is from friends and family. I received comments like: "Everyone turns to religion during stressful times, you are scared right now, it will pass." I was also told, "People are always using God as a crutch during hard times." Being a new Christian, this rattled me and initially had me uncertain about my decision. I did not understand it then, but what I was experiencing was the assault of the enemy and spiritual warfare. It was a battle I was not prepared for at that time. One thing you must remember is that when you decide to stop being a wanderer, you will face assaults from the enemy via family and friends. He will use them to attack your faith. I have been a Christian for 28 years now, and I would love to say that I lived in complete obedience to God and made no mistakes, but sadly this is not the truth. Since then, I have gone through various stages in my faith that has gotten me to where I choose to win in life through Christ. You may ask, "When is he going to get to the winning part?" All I can say is, have patience. Many of you that are reading this book fall in the following category:

- Confused about your identity
- Wandering around with no sense of direction or destination
- Have had a wilderness experience
- You are currently in the wilderness.

I will cover what I have experienced to get me where I am today. The Apostle Paul says it like this:

> *Brothers, I do not consider myself to have taken hold of it. But one thing I do: forgetting what is behind and reaching forward to what is ahead, I pursue as my goal the prize promised by God's heavenly call in Christ Jesus."*
> *Philippians 3:13-14 (HCSB)*

Just like Paul, I have not obtained, but I do choose to forget those things that are behind me. I choose to forget the wasted time and energy I spent living outside of God's grace. I do know that my wandering ended when I gave my heart to Jesus during Desert Storm.

INTO THE WILDERNESS

But the men who had gone up with him responded, "We can't go up against the people because they are stronger than we are!" Numbers 13:31 (HCSB)

Do not harden your hearts as in the rebellion, on the day of testing in the wilderness... Hebrews 3:8 (HCSB)

God allowed the children of Israel to wander in the desert after they challenged His faithfulness towards them. Like the children of Israel, we too can find ourselves in their position due to unbelief and doubt. There are also times when God will allow us to go through extreme trials to prepare us for His service. We are reminded of this when we observe the life of David's when he was pursued by King Saul. And Joseph, whose brothers sold him into slavery because they were jealous and envious of him. However, whatever series of events lands you in a wilderness experience, know that God's purpose is for you to come out as pure gold.

One of the first things that the Marine Corps does during boot camp is to strip you of your civilian ways. They immediately impose order and discipline by attempting to break you down so that they can rebuild you the way they want. They take your civilian clothes, shave all of your hair off, confiscate all jewelry, etc. All of your rights are stripped away, and you are identified by a number on your t-shirt. For three months of your life, you undergo one of the most grueling trainings on earth. They challenge you physically, mentally, and academically with the hopes of identifying the weak. The weak will undergo motivational reconditioning. If the reconditioning does not work, you will be released under an "Other than Honorable Discharge." Indeed the Marines are the "few, and the proud" as only a few out of each batch of recruits ever make it out of boot camp and earn the coveted title of Marine. You may be asking, why would anyone subject themselves to such abuse? For one, most recruits have no clue as to what they are in for before boot camp. Secondly, most recruits have a false sense of preparedness. They think everything they learned from the civilian world could help them make it through their training. It's not enough to be physically strong or academically experienced; the recruit must be disciplined, mentally sound, and willing to obey orders without protest. This is where most recruits fall short. The main goal is to prepare the recruit to be a well-disciplined fighting machine that will develop the endurance to persevere under extreme hardships to accomplish the assigned mission and purpose. As mentioned before, to achieve this, the recruit must be broken down, rebuilt, and prepared for duty. In some ways, God's approach to developing us for His service is not far from the above analogy. God does not use the devices of man. He takes us through His "refining fire," which may come through a wilderness experience. The Bible says that Jesus was led by the Spirit into the wilderness to be tested.[3] The children of Israel wandered for forty years in the wilderness because of their complaining and unbelief.[4] I ended the last chapter with my salvation experience. When I became a Christian, my days of wandering and being in bondage to sin was over. Still, I found myself wrestling and struggling in my salvation. A few Sundays before I left the Middle East after the Gulf War, a minister, preached a message out of the book of Joshua, chapter 24. In that chapter, Joshua is near death. He is delivering his last exhortation calling the people to complete obedience and service to God. Joshua boldly declares that he and his household will serve the Lord. The minister went on to say that our battle will start when we get back to the states where we would have access to devices that could cause us to compromise our faith. This puzzled me. For almost two years, I lived under the challenges and stress of war. The minister

---

[3] See Mathew 4:1 any version

[4] See Numbers 13 any version

also said that we had been shielded and isolated from these temptations being over in the Gulf. We did not have easy access to the pleasures of sin that America offers. In light of this, he urged us to choose who we were going to serve. Now in the back of my mind, I said to myself, "Not me, I am in it to win it." Let me backtrack a little right here.

Remember how I described the process that the Marine Corps took to ensure that the recruits were well-trained for war? Although I successfully completed boot camp, there were some aspects of the training I did not pay too much attention to. One was the NBC (Nuclear, Biological, and Chemical) training, which I showed a complete disregard for. After all, when I joined the Marines, fighting a war of any type was the furthest thing on my mind. So I did not see the point in paying too much attention to this part of the training. Before deploying to the Gulf, we were briefed that Sadaam was known for using chemical weapons, and there was a high probability that he would use them on us. As you can imagine, this did not sit well with me. Death by chemical weapons was known to be agonizing, and the victims usually suffered greatly before dying. Even if you survived a chemical attack, its effects are crippling and long-lasting. One night in September 1990, Sadaam launched several Scud missiles, potentially loaded with chemical weapons, at our camp. As the patriot missiles were knocking the scuds out of the sky, I was running in terror, trying to remember how to correctly put on my gas mask. The training I had neglected in boot camp crippled my knowledge, and I did not know what to do. Thank God there were no chemicals loaded in the scuds because if there were, I probably would not be here today. Had I chose to pay attention to my training, I would not have been unprepared, so it is when it comes to our spiritual life. We need to heed the instructions of God so that we can be prepared to face the fiery darts of the enemy. Obeying God's instructions safeguards us from the seductive draw of sin. The Bible says it like this:

> *Put on the full armor of God so that you can stand against the tactics of the devil. Ephesians 6:11 (HCSB)*

Nonetheless, I did not heed the warning the minister gave us before I left the Gulf. Just like Peter, who denied Christ three times, it did not take long before I started denying Christ in my lifestyle. Sure I went to church, but I lived in such compromise that the evidence of my salvation was not seen. Here's the kicker, unlike the times in Okinawa when the conviction of my sin would wear off; this time, it did not. I was miserable, and into the wilderness, I went. One thing about God, He will allow us to stay in the desert until we change or die. Yes, I said to die, either spiritually, physically, or both. God does not kill us, but our sinful choices surely will.

> *For the wages of sin is death, but the gift of God is eternal life in Christ Jesus our Lord. Romans 6:23 (HCSB)*

HAPPILY EVER AFTER

I met my wife, Keshah, in 1995. At the time we met, there was no romantic interest of any sort. She was an aspiring singer and a single mother of two children. I was a struggling music producer in a dying marriage, which ended in a nasty divorce. I was supposed to work with Keshah to help with her music career, but soon after we started dating. Now at this time, I was a broken man, and if my wife would have known our Pastor, then our Pastor would have told her I was not a prospect. She would have been correct. There was no evidence that I had a relationship with God or even knew who He was. Even though she knew of my divorce, she took a chance on me anyway. And, like most men, I tried impressing her with material things; elaborate trips and gifts for her two children. This cloak and dagger went on for some time—nonetheless, my real state of being started to reveal itself. My wife tells me that she had always seen something good in me, but looking back now, I think she was crazy to put up with what most women would have called a weak man. Somehow, I convinced her to marry me, and on September 8, 1996, we got married. It was bad enough that I was in a hard place in my mind, but to bring a woman and two innocent children into my mess was just awful. To the ladies that are reading this book, I know you have been told that if a man will not work and is not financially responsible, leave that man alone, he is not a prospect. I am telling you even if he does work and is financially responsible but does not love God or is in a backslidden state; leave that man alone as well. I was gainfully employed, had earned a degree in Electronics, but my mind and spiritual life were in turmoil. I unwisely included three more individuals into my tumultuous life. My wife had no idea what she was walking into.

We moved to Irving, Texas, a town just outside of Dallas. I was working at a premier semiconductor company. Our first apartment was a medium-sized, one-bedroom apartment that I did not have trouble paying before getting married. It did not take long before I realized that my income was not sufficient for a family of four. Keshah also did not know that a family of four could be so expensive. Before we were married, she received public assistance. Our first argument took place in a grocery store. She was placing items in the basket that she had usually purchased with federal aid, and I said, "Hey, we can't afford that." So I started replacing the items she put in the basket with generic brands. I did not care if they did not taste the same; I was thinking of affordability. We got into an argument. We laugh about that experience now, but back then, it was a big deal. As the reality of family life kicked in, both of us wondered about our decision to marry. Immediately, I started confiding in a friend whom my wife did not get along with. I began to complain and basically have a pity party about my situation. My complaining got so bad that even my friend's wife was disgusted with me in regards to how I spoke about my wife and family.

I never referred to my wife with cuss words, but I might as well have. After all, I asked Keshah to marry me. She thought that she was getting a prince, and instead, she got a wimp. She found herself caught in the hardships of my wilderness. One of the signs that a person is in the wilderness is complaining. And I did a lot of complaining. Most other women would have left me then, but she did not. I accused my wife of trapping me into taking all of the responsibility of caring for the children so that she could stay at home to chill. It was awful.

I was not leading my family spiritually. We did not attend church, and my paycheck would disappear before I even had a chance to see the money. I would come home from work, get on my music equipment, and would not pay any attention to my wife or my children. Keshah would get so upset, but even when she yelled at me, she never used profanity.

Neither did I. Despite not using profane words, the tension in our home was depressing and about to explode. I would often speak negatively and say things like, "We are doomed." or "Nothing can save us now, it's all over." One day I decided I had enough and was going to leave. I was so much a coward that I was planning to leave without saying anything. I was just going to take off and leave my wife and two small children with nothing and no way to take care of themselves. Thankfully, there was this still small voice that spoke to me. It was so faint that I could hardly recognize it, but after a while, I knew it was God. I got on my knees, and I prayed these exact words," Lord, I am about to do something foolish, and I need you to help me not to." So the following Sunday morning, I got up early, got myself and Marcus dressed and walked to this church called Open Arms Fellowship. The topic that morning was on building and strengthening families. That evening, I returned to the church with my wife Keshah, Marcus, and my daughter Constant.

HEALING IN THE WILDERNESS

Jody Nichols was the Pastor of "Open Arms Fellowship." He wasn't exactly a "fire and brimstone" preacher, but one could tell that he was a no-nonsense type of person. From the time my family joined Open Arms, Pastor Jody took a special interest in my family life. He could tell that I was struggling in my manhood and had no clue about being a Godly husband and father. He had enough experience and wisdom from God that he could tell we were in the wilderness of life and in need of some immediate intervention. One thing I have learned over the years is that my wife's behavior is directly proportional to where I am at spiritually. Pastor Jody and my current Pastor, Pastor Jacqueline Flowers, would continuously say this to me. Back then, I would get upset because I thought it was utterly unfair to place all of the pressure on me. After all, Keshah has a role to play in the marriage as well. She had flaws, too, right? The Bible says it like this:

> *Husbands, love your wives, just as Christ loved the church*
> *and gave Himself for her to make her holy, cleansing her*

with the washing of water by the Word. He did this to present the church to Himself in splendor, without spot or wrinkle or anything like that, but holy and blameless. In the same way, husbands are to love their wives as their own bodies. He who loves his wife loves himself. Ephesians 5:25-28 (HCSB)

This type of love and sacrifice requires a strong relationship with God because, without one, we men can be very selfish. I am no bible scholar, so I will not attempt to expound on the obvious message. It is a mandate from God that husbands are to love their wives and sacrifice their lives for them. I believe that our time at Open Arms Fellowship was the start of God, bringing us out of the wilderness. Although up to that point, I had been a professing Christian for seven years, and my wife, a preacher's kid her entire life. We never really learned how to experience God intimately. Like the children of Israel, when they were in the wilderness, God was shedding away the chaff while training and testing them. So that when they came out of the wilderness, they would not bring the same mindset and sinful ways into the Promised Land. Yes, sir, things were about to change, and just like in boot camp, the training began. God always starts with the head and the leadership when He starts to bring about change, especially in a marriage. The woman can pray until she is blue in the face, but change comes when the man changes or decides to put himself in the position to hear from God. Do not get me wrong, a praying woman is powerful. God hears their prayers, and things happen when a wife prays for her husband. A Godly woman's prayers are like catalysts to a formula God uses to get us, men, into position. So women, if your husband, son, nephew, etc. are out of place, just pray and watch God move. This was pretty much what my wife was doing behind the scenes before I decided to bring my family to church, but I had no clue she was doing this. Now, if my wife would have nagged me to go to church, I would have probably followed through with leaving my family.

Things started changing for our family, and Pastor Jody was God's instrument for that change. Pastor Jody is a kind man, and he cared about God's people but absolutely hated whining and complaining. Pastor Jody and his family became like our family, and we respected his no-nonsense persona. When he would counsel my wife and me, I used those sessions to vent and complain about my wife. At first, Pastor Jody tried to be empathetic; until one session, he let me have it. He told me to stop complaining and be a man. At first, I could not believe what I was hearing. He continued to scold me as if I was a child in the principal's office being reprimanded for misconduct. It was like the scene from the movie "The Godfather" when the god father's godson came to him, whining and the godfather shook him and told him to act like a man. I was furious, but I could not move a muscle. All I could do was sit there and take it. He led me through the scriptures about how a man should treat his wife from God's perspective. Looking back, I was blaming my problems on my wife. In essence, I blamed her for my wilderness. However, I was the one who dragged her in the mess I was already in. I would like to say that during our time at Open Arms Fellowship that I mastered loving my wife like Christ loves the church, but that would not be the truth. It took me several years to grow into the man I am today.

SPIRITUAL BOOT CAMP IN THE WILDERNESS

In 1998, the Asian stock market crashed, and many Asian businesses in America severely downsized or either closed shop altogether. Several of my colleagues, along with myself, had lost our jobs. Unlike times past, no recruiters were recruiting for premier employers. As usual, my wife was very positive and believing God for the best. Unfortunately, I was back to my naysaying and complaining and would get upset with my wife for not being down in the dumps like I was. One day, I decided to try it her way, so I went on a three day fast. I did not fast to find a job. I went on a fast so that I could focus on God and hear from him. I did come to a place of peace with God and whatever His will was for my family and me. The week after, I received a call from a recruiter for a high tech company in Minnesota. I made it past the first interview, and then I was flown to Minnesota for a second one and was made an unofficial offer. When I came back to Irving, I told my wife the good news, and my wife told everyone. I felt like I was Moses, and I was leading my family to the Promised Land.

I recalled in the book of Numbers when the spies came back from surveying the land. They all agreed that the land was fertile and very fruitful; however, the people that inhabited the land were well-established nations with seasoned military forces. Joshua and Caleb acknowledged this fact, but they had a different perspective than the other ten spies that accompanied them. The other spies mentioned to the Israelites that the land was good, but they could not defeat the people who occupied the land. Joshua and Caleb reminded the people that God was with them and was ready to fight and take the land. I am not justifying the unbelief of the ten spies, but I am the type of person who would like all of the facts before venturing out on a task I know nothing about. The interviews went well, and Minnesota seemed like a great place for families. However, my wife and I soon found out that there were a few challenges we did not foresee. Had we known about these challenges beforehand, we would not have moved. I have found that this is the beauty of God's nature and who He is. He does not give all of the details, and He is surely not oblivious to the challenges and risks that He allows us to be exposed to when He is perfecting us. Our church family gave us a nice going-away party, and we were on a euphoric high as we went forth in the blessings of God.

When we arrived in Minnesota, the temporary living quarters were two suite rooms at the Candle Wood Suites Hotel. Now imagine trying to keep two toddlers and a 9-year-old quiet in a place like that. Then, a week after moving to Minnesota, my new employer had closed the division of the company I was recruited for down. They had moved it back to R&D, and I, along with 100 other people, had lost their jobs. Now here we were, several thousand miles away from Texas, during winter and out of work again. We had no family or friends we could turn to, and our temporary living was coming to an end. By the grace of God, I was picked up by the parenting company. To my dismay, the circus did not stop there. In Texas, the wages I was being paid would have been excellent; however, in Minnesota, my wages were considered low income. Keshah and I found out that finding an apartment to accommodate a family of 5 was very difficult. In fact, the apartment availability for a three-bedroom was less than 2%, and with the temporary housing coming close to an end, our stress levels were very high. All of a sudden, our little Promised Land appeared to be filled with thorns and thistles. I asked the Human Resources for a housing extension, and thank God they approved the extension on our temporary living condition. However, later that week, I was involved in a car accident, and our car was totaled. Though the accident was not my fault, we had no money in the bank to put down on a new car, let alone to pay for a rental. In the midst of it all, God showed His faithfulness. The insurance company paid our car off and gave us $1000 cashback. We were able to buy groceries and go car shopping. Now my wife, since the beginning of our relationship, had a very high taste of living. I made the fatal mistake of asking her which car she wanted.

When we got to the car lot, as usual, she chose the best minivan on the showroom floor. I stared at here with this, "Are you crazy?" look, and she shrugged and said, "You asked me which car I wanted, and I want that one." When the salesmen came over, I knew there was no way that we were going to get approved for the car. I was very upfront with the salesman and told him all we had was 500 dollars and nothing more. He told me, "Okay, no problem." To my surprise, we were approved. But we had to wait until the next day to sign the paperwork because the department had closed. He told us to take the car and that they would call us when all of the paperwork was ready. God came through again in a big way! Despite everything, God chose to give us the best! I am not saying that the only way God shows His faithfulness is through the acquisition of material things. Please do not take that from the experience I am sharing. Many times I have experienced God without the manifestation of material goods. Often God would provide peace and strength in my inner man to keep believing He is who He says He is.

MANNA IN THE WILDERNESS

One thing I have learned is that God loves to bless His children. His blessing is not meant for us to become like spoiled children. But depending on where we are in Him, these blessings will help increase our faith, help in times of need, experience His love and bless others. While we were living in temporary housing and before the car accident,

Keshah and I sought a church so that we could draw strength from being around the saints of God. We looked in the yellow pages for a church that had a name that sounded like a non-denominational church. Now back in 1998, only the privileged had the internet, and there was no such thing as "Smartphone's," so the yellow pages had to do. Our search led us to The Church upon the Rock. That Sunday, we loaded up the family and found our way to the church with the directions scribbled on a piece of paper and a map of Minnesota. Being from Texas and coming from a multicultural non-denominational church in Irving, we expected to find the same thing. Our initial encounter was not so.

When we arrived at the church, we did not see one black, brown, or yellow face, and everyone stared at us when they got out of their cars. We stayed in the car for about 30 minutes before we decided to go inside the church. Now when we went inside, we were greeted with a warm, sincere welcome. The people were so friendly and genuinely sincere. I must admit I breathed a sigh of relief when I saw a brother singing in the choir. After the service was over, several of the members invited us to their homes to fellowship. Being so far away from home, this was such a blessing as we were starving for fellowship with other Christians. That day, we made several friendships that we still hold dear today. We always cherish friends like Ben & Ruth Lee, Ray, and Mom Sue, the Bayer family, Mark, and Karen Warner, the Myerson family, and many more. This was just one way God provided us with manna in the form of fellowship and relationships.

Though we just experienced a great blessing with the new car, my pay still did not cover all of our needs. In fact, the new car payment was 80 dollars less than our previous one that was totaled in the wreck. We did not overextend ourselves. We actually improved our living expenses by 80 bucks. We were a one-income family, and my wife was pregnant with our son, Joshua. Most of our income was spent on rent, utilities, and doctor bills. There was barely enough for food or clothing for all of us. During this time, we frequently visited the food and clothing bank at the Catholic Diocese. This was a very humbling experience for us, and my ego took a massive hit.

I felt like a failure, a beggar, and many ways a loser. Thank God for my wife, who reminded me daily in more ways than one that I was her king, and she loved me and was in my corner. I believe God uses experiences like this to purge us of pride and to teach us to depend on His provision. There is one particular woman I remember from a local charity organization. Her name was Joe Buchanan, and she was an instrument that God used to make His provision possible. She gave us gas cards, food vouchers, and access to the food bank. I was still battling with pride and had my wife do all of the callings when we needed something. Sometimes this would cause my wife's respect level for me to waver a bit. Husbands listen to me, nothing kills a woman's sense of stability faster than a man who is full of pride and lacks strength. A woman can handle hard times if she sees her husband standing strong and willing to take the blows to his ego if it means that his family is taken care of. She will build you up when you come home so that you can go back out the next day and handle your business. I did not know it then, but God was purging those things out of me, as well as my wife, that would have hindered us today. Today, I can say that when it comes to seeking out what is best for my family, I go out with the power and might of God to make it happen. My wife makes whatever I bring home sustainable for our family. She does not have to worry about negotiating with me and convincing me to understand what is needed for our household.

When we moved back to Texas, God had laid it on Ms. Buchanan's heart to give us gas cards for the trip back. God even used our landlord at Lakeview Commons to bless us. It was around Christmas time, and we wanted to drive to Texas to visit our family. We did not have the money, and we did not want to ask Ms. Buchanan because driving to Texas was a want, not a need. We settled on spending Christmas in Minnesota again. We went to pay for our rent, and our landlord asked us what we were doing for Christmas. We told her that we were staying at home. She wished us a Merry Christmas and said we could use that month's rent money to buy our children gifts. She gave us permission to pay our rent after Christmas.

We ended up using the money not only to buy gifts for our children but to drive to Texas to spend Christmas with our family. There were so many incredible ways God provided for us. I am not trying to sound superficial. God's provision goes beyond just our physical needs.

Nevertheless, He literally supplied all of our needs and even some of our wants. My wife, like most black women, likes to get her hair done. We could not afford this expense. To be truthful, I wanted my wife to be able to treat herself since she was a stay-at-home mother. My wife befriended a lady that stayed in our apartments that happened to be a hairdresser. She made a deal with my wife that if she watched her son after he came home from school, she would do her hair for free every week. I was so happy for my wife! Getting her hair done was an opportunity for her to have "me time" at the end of the week and to feel beautiful. I particularly enjoyed seeing her happy feeling beautiful. Jesus says:

> *So don't worry, saying, 'What will we eat?' or 'What will we drink?' or 'What will we wear?' Mathew 6:31 (HCSB)*

I remember one Sunday, while we lived in Minnesota, we did not have gas to go to our church, so we went to one close by. When offering time came, all we had was a nickel. I was too embarrassed to give it, but God kept nudging at my heart to give it, so I did. I tried to put my hand deep in the offering bag so that no one would know that all I had was a nickel. I am not sure if God displayed His sense of humor or if it was my imagination. But that nickel seemed to have made the loudest sound as it fell into the offering bag. My wife and I sunk in our seats, hoping no one else heard it. The next day, one of the church members came over and blessed us with over 400 dollars' worth of groceries. We did not tell anyone that we didn't have money or money for food. We didn't even let off a vibe that we needed anything. Now, as a man, I enjoyed providing for my family, and it was hard for me to accept gifts. I felt like I should have been able to take care of my responsibilities. God allowed us to be in that place, and He took care of us. God has to bring us to a place where we have no one but Him. He allows us to experience certain events in our lives that will burn away the chaffs.

F O U R
THE HARD PLACES

They reported to Moses: "We went into the land where you sent us. Indeed it is flowing with milk and honey, and here is some of its fruit. However, the people living in the land are strong, and the cities are large and fortified. We also saw the descendants of Anak there. Numbers 13:27-28 (HCSB)

M y Pastor has said on numerous occasions that we grow in the hard places. She has also said that we should be in the company of people that challenge us. If a person wants to become better, they must be put through training that is challenging. Now the flip side to this is that if one buckle under the pressure of the challenge and gives up, they will never accomplish their goal and taste victory. My son, Marcus, asked me why the people who were in other military branches have to attend boot camp again if they want to join the Marines. But a former Marine that desires to cross over to a different branch does not. In three words, I told him, "It's our training." We are not called the "Few and the Proud" for nothing.

In 1999, I interviewed with a premier semiconductor Company in Austin, Texas. They flew me down, and I nailed the interview. I was offered the job on the spot, complete with stock options. Just like the company in Minnesota, they paid for the move and gave us housing accommodations in a plush place. God was with us. Before our move, on our last Sunday at "Church upon the Rock," they gave us a going away blessing. That particular Sunday, there was a visiting evangelist that prophesied over us. Now, I was not big on the prophesy thing back then as I saw it only as something done in the Old Testament of the bible and not relevant for the present day.

I went along with the evangelist, but in my heart, I was not buying it. I was not convinced at all. Despite my unbelief, there was one thing that stuck out about what she said. She said that amid God's blessing, we were going to face more challenging times and do not be afraid because God is going to get us through it. I admit I was a little startled. In the back of my mind, I was thinking that there was no such thing as a modern prophet. So I dismissed what was said. We made our move to Austin, and I once again felt like Moses. My wife and I were speaking faith. We felt as if we had arrived, and all of our dreams were about to come true. We started looking at houses; after all, my new income was more than enough. I attended my training courses and did reasonably well. Things were going great. To my disappointment, when I was released from training, this incredible and perfect job started to turn sour almost immediately. My new coworkers were not very friendly, and they made it their chief aim to point out my weaknesses and mistakes.

There were so many explosive egos and pride in that environment that if methane gas were present, the smallest spark would have caused it to violently explode. Needless to say, I was very intimidated. Once again, I quickly shrank into a ball of low self-esteem. I felt like I could not do anything right. I was ridiculed continuously on the job. At first, I was made fun of behind my back; then, they started doing it openly. I was so incompetent at my job that they stopped assigning me systems to work on, and no one wanted to work with me. I was willing to work, but I allowed myself to be so intimidated by my coworkers that I was literally dysfunctional. My wife knew that something was not right because I stopped talking about how great my work was. I avoided talking about work altogether. This bothered her because she had seen this side of me before. She had seen the fear, intimidation, mood swings, etc., but she could not do for me what I was not willing to do for myself. I had to trust and depend on God. You see, just like God knew that He was sending the spies from Israel to spy on pretty intimidating civilizations. God knew what I was going to face long before I got there. I cannot say enough that God allows us to face challenges in life so that our faith and dependence on Him would grow. Anyone who aspires to be great must face challenges. I believe even before the spies were chosen, God knew what they would do. A lot of times, people will treat us based upon how we see ourselves, and our life will be guided by the course of our thought life. The ten spies described themselves as such:

> *We even saw the Nephilim there — the descendants of Anak come from the Nephilim! To ourselves we seemed like grasshoppers, and we must have seemed the same to them. Numbers 13:33 (HCSB)*

Now, none of the spies had spoken to any of the people in the city. They were spying, which means they were surveying the land without being seen. How could they have known what the people thought of them? The spies panicked and brought fear into the minds and hearts of the Israelites. They were so afraid that they were willing to go back to Egypt and commit to being slaves again. I will not expound on how this angered God, but I will say this. Chances are the inhabitants of the land heard about the Israelites and how God delivered Israel from Egypt, the baddest boys on the block. They were probably terrified they would suffer the same fate if they tried going up against Israel.

Most of the time, we bring about our own ill will by what we think and say about ourselves. Notice that the spies with the negative report said that they were as grasshoppers in their own sight. They felt low of themselves, and consequently, they were also saying that the inhabitants of that land and the gods they served were mightier than the God they served. They totally dismissed how God miraculously delivered them from Egypt. And so it was in my life when I was facing significant challenges with my employer during that time. I saw myself as small, dumb, and insignificant. And that's how my coworkers viewed me. Not only did I suffer, but I brought unnecessary suffering on my family as well. I plunged us into a spiritual and economic free fall. I became irritable with my wife and children and began to neglect them as I became consumed with self-pity and fear.

On Friday, September 14, 2001, I was laid off from my job. We quickly spent whatever savings we had and my 401k. We ended up having to move in with my wife's grandfather. To make matters worse, we lost that beautiful van God had given us in Minnesota. Within a year, we went from the mountain top to the valley. What happened? What happened was that I took my eyes off the Father and started paying attention to the storms of life around me. We were in a hard place. It was only God's grace that kept my wife, that incredible woman, from leaving me. When we walk in fear and get out of line with God, we start making irrational and downright stupid decisions. Look what the children of Israel did when they heard the bad report from the ten spies:

> *So they said to one another, "Let's appoint a leader and go back to Egypt. Numbers 14:4 (HCSB)*

Wow, what a terrible idea. Just like the Israelites, I came up with a bad idea of my own. I tried to pursue a career as a Gospel rapper at the age of 30, with 4 children, a wife, and no income. My, how foolish. My wife went along with it because she wanted to support me. However, I could see the fear and look of uncertainty in her eyes as I caused my family to suffer even more. During this time, I had no wise counselor at least someone to point out to me that what I was doing was not of God. My father-in-law did try to intervene by hiring me as a part-timer in his construction company. Reality did not hit me until my family had to move out of my wife's cousin duplex, and we were going to be homeless. Out of desperation, we moved to Alvin, Texas. The leadership at the church we attended at the time told us that this move was ordained by God and that we needed to "Move with the Cloud." I moved in the hope of finding a miracle that would help my family. When I arrived, Alvin was far from being a miracle. I moved there first, and my family ended up following me three months later. My wife and children stayed with our friends, Toussaint and Jackie Smith, in Sugarland, TX, while I lived in Alvin. The only time we could see or talk to each other was on Sunday because neither Keshah nor I had cell phones.

I managed to find employment at a grocery store, and eventually, my family was able to get an apartment. Things weren't the best, but we were able to manage at least for a little while. The move to Alvin was turning more into a nightmare with a series of unfortunate events.

My eldest daughter started getting into a lot of trouble in school and then eventually ran away from home. The police were useless. They showed little to no concern about finding her. During this time, my biological father had passed away. With all of this stress on me, I ended up having a nervous breakdown on my job. It led to my immediate termination and a lifetime ban from being employed there ever again. Once again, I found myself unemployed and my family one step away from being homeless. My spiritual life seemed even more null and void, and I stopped regularly attending church. I had ceased from being an adequate covering for my wife and family because I was not allowing Christ to be my head. I was giving satan free reign to wreak havoc on my family. What we must understand, especially us men, is that Satan is no match for God. However, if he can destroy and discredit God's creation, he will stop at nothing until this is accomplished. As the man of my home, I have the charge to serve and protect. When I abandon my post, I allow all that I am responsible for serving and protecting to be overrun by spiritual thieves and murderers.

During the Gulf War, I had to stand guard duty to ensure that the enemy would not sneak up on us by surprise. Often times, the Corporal of the Guard would test our alertness, especially during the late-night hours and early morning times. His approach was different, but his motives were the same. Sometimes he would try to sneak up on us or send an officer our way to get past us without proper authentication. Other times, he would simply come in a friendly manner to try to distract us from our duties. Some of these encounters could get pretty intense and hard to recognize. As the standing guard, the only person we were allowed to answer to is the Commanding Officer, Officer of the Day, officers and non-commissioned officers of the guard only. It did not matter if a four-star general came to us and commanded us to leave our post. It was the guard's duty to stand his ground until given a change of orders from the officers of the guard only.

As soldiers for Christ, God has given us general orders in His word. We are instructed to take on the whole armor of God to fight against our adversary, the devil.[5] Although this charge is given to all Christians,

---

[5] See Ephesians 6: 13~18

male and female, it is vitally important that we husbands and fathers are carrying out God's general orders.

THE TURN-AROUND

Sometime in 2004, Toussaint and Jackie Smith invited my wife and me to attend our current church home, Time of Celebration Ministries Church of Houston, TX. Back then, it was called From the Heart Ministries. We were still living in Alvin, TX, and my wife was still actively attending our former church. I had stopped attending church. My wife had convinced me to visit From the Heart Ministries. So the one Sunday, we made our way to the service. The church membership was much smaller than what we came from, and the praise and worship were not as extravagant, but the preaching was phenomenal.

I admit I was a little shocked that the pastor was a woman, Pastor Jacqueline T. Flowers. I had never seen a female pastor before. I was just a little surprised, but I did not have a problem with it. Although the sermon was excellent, I was not sold on attending church there. I felt that I had made so many bad choices that God was done with me and my lot in life was to suffer. After all, I made terrible choices, and now I had to pay the consequences for them. My thinking was very warped, and I believe that my wife was just hanging on by a thread. I never abused my wife in any way, physically or verbally. Still, the way I viewed life was literally choking the life out of her. My wife, by nature, is a kind and encouraging person.

My wife always saw the positives in my life. I often joke with her by saying that she can bring joy to a corpse. As I mentioned before, my Pastor often suggests that a man's wife's behavior is directly proportional to his. Also, as I admitted, that statement would upset me, even though deep down in my soul, I knew this to be true. In her book, "Where Are the Men." Pastor Flowers says, "The father extracts the best out of the wife and the best out of the children." [6]. At that time in my life, I was extracting the worst out of my family.

---

[6] Pastor Jacqueline T Flowers, *Where are the Men*, 1st ed. (Tamarac, FL: Llumina Christian Books, 2011), pg99

My family started attending From the Heart Ministries of Houston regularly. One Sunday, I decided to join. Before our joining, Pastor Flowers showed a genuine interest in my family. She was aware of where I was mentally and where my family was financially but never treated us indifferently. Pastor Flowers and Reverend Jerry Flowers, Sr., her husband, counseled my wife and me. Together they did their best to help our family holistically get back on track. Just like Pastor Jody Nichols, Pastor Flowers is a no-nonsense type of person, but she was kind and patient with us.

One of the things I noticed about the members of that church, especially the families, they seemed grounded in their faith. The men led their families with humility and were affectionate toward their wives. Usually, I can tell when someone is being fake and phony, but these guys were the real deal. I did not say much. I watched them, and the more I watched them, the more I wanted to become like them. At this time, I had obtained a job at the local cable company, and everything appeared to be turning around. The pay was not much, but it was closer to what I was earning when I was an electronic technician. I was able to keep gas in our car so that we could go to church, and we were able to catch up on some of our bills. After I was on the job for a month, I found that being a cable guy was not very easy. I have a degree in electronics, but for some reason, I could not meet the speed requirements for installing cable in the clients' homes. I was averaging 3 clients per day but was expected to do 6 to 8 minimum. I could not understand why this was so difficult for me when I had experience with troubleshooting complex electrical machinery.

The company ended up firing me before my 90 day probation period. "Here we go again.", I thought to myself. Satan began to taunt my thoughts. It was utter mental madness, and once again, I felt like a failure. I was back to feeling like I let my family down and that I could not do anything right. The difference this time was that I kept going to church. Some days I would go off by myself at our apartments and cry. I did not know what to do. I worked day labor jobs to keep food on our table. I tried to get back on with my previous employer, but they were not hiring. I decided to get my CDL license and drive a school bus. One day, I received a phone call from a former coworker that I met in training while working at the cable company, Kapila Zelinski. He told me about a company he worked for that built unmanned submarines. They were looking for someone who had electronics experience, and he had told them about me. He gave me their contact information, and I sent them my resume. I was scheduled for an interview immediately. The meeting appeared to have gone well, but several weeks went by, and I still had not heard anything from them. I eventually lost hope that I would get an offer and was prepared to settle for the bus driving position. At the time, I was at the end of my school bus training and had my final ride along with a bus driver whose route I was getting ready to take over. The behavior of the children on the bus was absolutely ridiculous. I did not think I could be a school bus driver and have to deal with the attitudes of those children. To make things worse, I had found out that trainees are not paid during training. Again our rent was due, we needed food, we were absolutely broke.

One day I was riding my bike home for lunch, and Adrian Carrillo, a former co-worker of mine, stopped me. He put my bike in his car trunk and gave me a ride home. Adrian was also a born again Christian. He was strong in his faith and believed in the power of prayer. Adrian also believed in the prophetic word. He proceeded to tell me that God was getting ready to do something incredible in my life, but I must not lose heart; just trust in Jesus. We arrived at my apartments, and before I got out of the car, he prayed for me. I was grateful for his prayers. Still, I planned to move back to Austin and beg my mother for a place to stay until we got on our feet. I was very desperate and did not care if every ounce of my dignity was lost. I had to get my family into a safe place in a hurry, or so I thought. One of the things the enemy tries to do is to get us to give up right before the major breakthrough from God happens. The bible says it like this:

> *You rejoice in this, though now for a short time you have had to struggle in various trials so that the genuineness of your faith — more valuable than gold, which perishes though refined by fire — may result in praise, glory, and honor at the revelation of Jesus Christ. Peter 1:6-7 (HCSB)*

It is during these hard places that we either progress or regress. I had a choice; I could have been like the children of Israel and went back to Austin with my tail between my legs or stand and fight. My options were not good. On the one hand, my family was facing complete financial ruin on the other total ridicule and accusation if I returned to Austin to live with my mother. After lunch, I returned to the bus training facility to finish up my shift, I had no intention of returning the next day. On my way home, I began thanking God for His goodness. For no particular reason, I just started thanking Him, confessing my sin and asking for forgiveness for not trusting in Him. I did not ask Him for anything, though I needed much. I just wanted to talk to my heavenly Father.

After a while, I forgot about my problems and was having a good time talking to God. I was talking aloud, and I am sure the cars passing by me probably thought I was crazy, but I did not care. I found myself overtaken by a peace that could only come from God. I said to the Lord, "Your will be done even if it means more hard times." I was not giving up.

On the contrary, I was surrendering to God. I had spent so much time trying to figure out how to direct my path instead of letting God do it for me. I started feeling hopeful. I decided to go to the day labor the next day so that I could earn a little quick cash to buy groceries for my family. I do not want to over-spiritualize my experience. I was still very aware of the possibility of my family being homeless again. Although I was experiencing the peace of God, Satan did not stop taunting my thoughts

Many of us have heard the term, "God moves in mysterious ways." Well, this phrase is nowhere in the bible, but there are many passages in the holy text that implies it. Soon after I was finished praying, God moved mysteriously on my behalf. A Human Representative from the company, I thought, had forgotten about me, called, and offered me a position. I nearly swerved off the road into a ditch while riding my bicycle when I heard the news. Not only did this position pay well, but it was a direct-hire with full benefits. As I reflect back on this event while I am writing this book, I am finding it hard to fight back the tears of joy and thankfulness.

The enemy really attacks us hard when the breakthrough is close.

Whether the breakthrough is mental, spiritual, financial, or all three, it's all the same; the enemy wants to get us to give up. I could hear the devil telling me, "You might as well give up, nothing's going to work out for you or your family. You are a failure. You can't do anything right." In life, we will experience various seasons, some for the better and some for the worse. Make no mistake, the enemy will be there roaring like a lion trying to frighten and devour your hope. Though God had given my family a great blessing, the enemy did not slow down his assaults and attacks. I was only able to withstand them with God's power to resist. I believed what God said and not the lies of the enemy. The bible says:

> *Be serious! Be alert! Your adversary the devil is prowling around like a roaring lion, looking for anyone he can devour. I Peter 5:8 (HCSB)*

The enemy roars loud to get us to make irrational decisions based on our emotions. He studies us. His tactics are tailor-made to our habits, thoughts, and the words we speak. The enemy's plan is to get us to doubt and lose confidence in God, which leads to our complete demise. Another thing I must mention is that it is good to have a strong support group of faithful Christians. When Adrian Carrillo prayed for and spoke life to me, it gave me the encouragement I needed. Before seeing him, I was right on the verge of quitting. The bible calls it "iron sharpening iron." The Scripture also tells us:

> *If you faint in the day of adversity, your strength is small. Proverb 24:10 (NKJV)*

My strength was small, so I had to rely on Christ's power. I was not strong enough to handle the fight. God, being rich in mercy, came to me and my family's rescue with the new job, I was now able to provide for them. My dignity was restored, and we moved away from Alvin, TX, and closer to my new place of employment.

> *When the enemy comes in like a flood, the Spirit of the Lord will lift up a standard against him." Isaiah 59:19B (NKJV)*

FIVE
PRAY OR PREY

You ask and do not receive, because you ask amiss, that
you may spend it on your pleasures. James 4:3 (NKJV)

When I became a Christian, I did not understand how vital a stable prayer life was. Sure, I heard other Christians say that to be strong in the faith, I must develop a healthy prayer life. As a new Christian, this all sounded foreign to me. Questions raced through my mind, such as "What should I pray about?" and "Who should I pray for?" Over time, I eventually developed a consistent prayer life. What I learned along the way was that even when we pray, we could still become susceptible and fall prey to the tactics of satan.

After several years of being a professed Christian, I still had a problem with believing God with issues and concerns I had prayed to Him about. I would pray, then worry and pretty much doubt that what I prayed about would be answered. I was afraid that God would say no or that His answers would always be no. Though sometimes God will say 'no' to some of our requests, I was battling with a trust issue. I would get upset with God because I did not receive what I had prayed for. I would ask God to help me, but I didn't think He could. I would even try to "spiritualize" it. For example, early in my marriage, I would drive my wife crazy by making comments like "I know God can, but would He do it for me?" The bible says:

> *But let him ask in faith, with no doubting, for he who*
> *doubts is like a wave of the sea driven and tossed by the*
> *wind. James 1:6 (NKJV)*

I wasted so many years living with that mindset and brought unnecessary suffering to my wife and children. As I mentioned in the last chapter, I had experienced a turn around when the posture of my heart changed. I knew that if God did not intervene on me and my family's behalf, we would be in big trouble. The funny thing is that while I was praising God on my way home from the bus depot, I did not ask for anything but for His forgiveness. I started thanking Him for what I did have, though, I knew I didn't know how I was going to take care of my family. God moved when I started believing that He would move for me. I trusted Him with my prayers, and He answered them. I could have cursed, but then I knew that the alternative would have been worse. I was able to choose His way and started thanking Him for His goodness. He brought to my remembrance all of the times He provided for my family many times before. I knew that my situation may not have changed at that moment, but my only choices were to pray and believe or become prey for the enemy.

When I started the new job at the electronics company, I really had to pray and believe God every step of the way. I've heard it said that a lesson not learned from will continually be repeated until the lesson is learned. All my life, I have struggled with low self-esteem, which developed into an inferiority complex. When I became a Christian, God allowed me to be in situations where I would come face-to-face with that beast called inferiority. I know it was His attempt to get me to rely on Him and to become confident in His power and not my own. I would fail the test repeatedly and buckle under the pressure. Once again, I found myself in the company of some of the brightest yet most self-absorbed people like I had encountered while working at the semiconductor company years earlier. On my first day of work, several of them made no apologies about letting me know how they felt about my being there. At that moment, I had a choice to make. Do I stand or do I buckle under the pressure? This time I decided to fight, not with my hands but in prayer, and honestly believe that God would fight my battles. This was not an easy task as I was faced with offensive behavior, even by those who professed to be Christians. The experience had me always on my knees and in the face of God. I would write scriptures out on cards and read them to myself in the men's restroom. Psalms 91 and Psalms 27 were my favorite go-to scriptures. It is one thing to read a passage and say, "That was inspirational." And it is a whole different thing when the words you read are literally the only thing keeping you from losing it.

God's Word is full of examples of men and women who had to face challenging times, especially those who were called and chosen by God. Take, for instance, King David; he was anointed by Samuel the prophet to be king in place of Saul. I genuinely believe that the word got around that David had been anointed as the successor to the throne, and he probably had some secret haters in his community. David's own brothers even rebuked him when he expressed disdain with the Philistines' champion, Goliath, who was threatening Israel. David probably felt that he was on his way to the top after slaying Goliath, yet instead, he spent years running for his life away from King Saul. It wasn't until Saul and his son's death many years later from the time Samuel first anointed David, that he was crowned king over Israel. It was in David's "in-between time" when he was a fugitive that he learned humility, leadership, and total reliance upon God through much prayer and supplication.

Gideon is another example. God called Gideon a "mighty man of valor," but when he was called, he was in a cave threshing wheat, hiding from the Midianites. Gideon even tried to explain to God why he was not the man for the job. Gideon questioned God and asked about all those miracles he grew up hearing about. He asked God if He was going to save Israel from their new enemies. God told him yes and that He was going to use Gideon to do it. Then Gideon replied with a "What are you talking about, Willis?" type of tone. Of course, I'm paraphrasing Gideon's encounter with God in my own words for the sake of simplicity. Just like King David, God handpicked Gideon to deliver his people from oppression. The interesting part of the story is that God allowed Gideon to face some insurmountable odds while on his journey to fulfill his purpose. These incidents drove Gideon to his knees before God, asking for clarity of the task God wanted him to complete. By the end of his trek, we see Gideon being transformed from a fearful soul into a magnificent leader and warrior. I have found that when I am faced with impossible challenges, prayer, praise, and worship to God always levels the playing field. Just like David, Gideon, and many others in the bible, prayer, and dependence upon God's power are crucial to navigating through life. When God allowed Job to be afflicted by Satan, Job's wife said to him:

> *Do you still hold fast to your integrity? Curse God and die! Job 2:9 (NKJV)*

Now the bible does not mention too much about Job's wife before or after this comment. Still, at the point where she and Job needed to be united as one, she chose to buckle under the pressure of the horrendous things happening to them. Job responds to his wife by calling her behavior foolish and decided not to sin or turn from God because of his affliction. It is also apparent that Job's wife did not have the same type of faith in God as Job did. If she had, I believe God would have referred to both of them as his faithful servants and not just Job. From the outside looking in, it is easy to frown upon Job's wife for her lack of faith in God in the face of adversity. As I look back over my own life, I have made the same fatal mistake as Job's wife and found myself in a vicious loop of spiritual impotence. The deciding factor between success and failure while walking with God is a vibrant prayer life. Is developing a stable prayer life easy? Well, that depends upon perspective. Are we asking from God's perspective or men? God is so gracious that He helps us in our areas of weakness, but He does not force us. The choice to believe Him and His promises are always up to us. Now, God's help may not always be viewed as help, especially when we are in the middle of hardships and what appears to be impossible challenges.

I am not saying that God exclusively allows us to experience hard times to get us to pray, but again, this is not always the case. Think of it as a relationship between a coach and an athlete. If the coach allows the athlete to train the same way all of the time, the athlete would peak and grow no further than their current training. So like any good coach, they change up the training regiment to bring out the best in the athlete. The changes could be more resistant, or interval training, but all are administered to work muscles that are generally not used to maximize the athlete's performance. The athlete can either reject or accept the new regiment; the choice is theirs. But unlike the earthly coach, God will not give up on us. He will just allow us to keep repeating the lesson until we learn and grow. When it comes to prayer, God is not impressed with elaborate or wordy prayers. He wants the "meat and potatoes." Sincere prayer can be as simple as "Help me." God is more interested in the posture of our hearts. He knows about our issues. He alone knows how to move us to a position for peak performance, and prayer is the vehicle to make things happen. The psalmist says:

> *In my distress I cried to the Lord, And He heard me.*
> *Psalm 120:1 (NKJV)*

I believe that because God allowed me and my family to experience hardship, it caused me to cry out to Him. I had to repeat lessons several times because of my lack of belief and inability to grow beyond the obstacles I faced. The crazy thing is that the exam God allowed me to repeat was the same one every single time. As I said earlier, my issue has always been low self-esteem. I would let myself get easily intimidated by people with strong, aggressive personalities and adverse events beyond my control. I'd shut down. In 2006, I had enough of failing and causing my family to be disadvantage spiritually and economically. When God allowed me to face the same challenges at my job, I hit my knees, strengthen myself in God, and focused on Him. He had been faithful to me even when I was at my worst.

By far, King David is my favorite character in the Old Testament, and I am sure this is true for many people who have read the bible. In I Samuel 30, the Amalekites had raided Ziklag, David's home, while David and his men were away. When David and his men returned home, they found the camp in ruins, their families missing along with all of the goods and livestock. In an instant, David goes from hero to zero, and his men wanted to stone him. I cannot imagine the type of stress that David must have been under. The most exciting part of the story wasn't that they were able to recover all of what they had lost. Still, it was David's attitude when he approached God about the situation. Instead of rushing in and asking God to help him recover all that they had lost, the bible says he encouraged himself in the Lord first. David had a praise party by himself first, and then he asked God the strangest thing:

So David inquired of the Lord, saying, "Shall I pursue this troop? Shall I overtake them?" And He answered him, "Pursue, for you shall surely overtake them and without fail recover all. 1 Samuel 30:8 (NKJV)

What a request! In my humanity, I would have begged God to help me get my family, along with my men's families, back and to give us the victory while doing so. David's request implies that If by any chance God would have said don't pursue, he wouldn't have. David trusted God, even if it meant never seeing his family again and face being murdered by his men. David was in between a rock in a hard place, but he trusted God's faithfulness, wisdom, and direction more than his own instinct. I believe this is how God wants us to be. God wants us to trust Him whether we are having great success or facing impending doom.

While my story does not compare to David's life, this is where I was during the summer of 2006 on my way home from the bus training facility. We had no money for rent or food; I was riding a bike, and my wife's job didn't pay much. I had to encourage myself in the Lord, and God moved on behalf of my family. Even after I was hired at my new job. God had allowed me to face the same giants that had defeated me time and time again in my past. I was able to overcome them because I had learned that praise and prayer are the keys to victory. I have not arrived, and I still face challenges, but I am determined to trust that my God will supply all of my needs according to His riches and glory.

S I X

THE HELP MEET

And the Lord God said, It is not good that the man should be alone; I will make him an help meet for him. Genesis 2:18 (KJV)

God knew the importance of providing a helper (a wife) for a man so that as husband and wife, the two can fulfill God-given purpose. Let me say up front that I am explicitly opposed to marital unions outside the confines of biblical truth and principle. I do understand that my position does not line up with today's popular culture and, in some cases, with people who say they are Christians as well. I also understand that "help meet" in Genesis 2:18 was primarily directed towards Adam's wife Eve. However, I want to expand on the "helpmeet" principle to describe the importance of Godly families and friends in a believer's life. With that being said, I want to take a little time to tell you about my helpmeet, my wife, Keshah Walker.

My wife is one of the kindest and loving people you would ever meet. She has never cursed me, shown disrespect, or put me down in over the 20 plus years we have been married. She had always built me up and encouraged me, even when I was not such a pleasant person to be around. I remember one day, I walked in on a conversation about wives and girlfriends that my co-workers were having. The way that some of those men talked about their wives saddened me as I could not relate to their situation. The conversations were infused with vulgarities and selfishness. Before I went into the judgmental mode, God allowed me to remember how I was towards my wife at the beginning of our marriage. I have never cursed my wife or spoke profanely towards her, but I did do a lot of complaining. I complained to my family and so-called friends about the pettiest things concerning her and basically exploited her weaknesses instead of amplifying her strengths. Without a single physical punch, I beat her down, and all the while, she kept building me up. When I had time to process what I had put my wife through, I prayed for those men. I did not point a judgmental finger at them because I remembered that I knew what it was like to be in their shoes. The bible says:

> *He who finds a wife finds a good thing, and obtains favor*
> *from the Lord. Proverbs 18:22 (NKJV)*

To the ladies that are reading this book, maybe it's your Boaz; you are his good thing. One of the major problems I see today is that we do not value our spouses and what they have to offer in the relationship. Too often, the things we value are superficial and lack the depth to cultivating healthy, Christ-centered, and purpose-driven marriages. We, as a people, have a tendency to look at the outer appearance instead of inner qualities. We are bent on focusing on the size of a paycheck and sexual performance in the bedroom as opposed to real intimacy. In today's society, sex sells, and commitment fails. I do not have any statistical data or quantifying numbers to back my claims. Still, it is not hard to find all types of performance enhancement drugs advertised on TV or in magazines claiming to give you the best sex of your life. We are also inundated with articles offering tips on how to be a better lover. We are also bombarded by sexual images on the cover of magazines in the checkout aisle at the local supermarket, billboards, commercials, and more. From my experience, I rarely see anything in mainstream media that promotes Godly relationships and purpose-driven marriages. The bible says:

> *And the Lord God said, It is not good that the man should*
> *be alone; I will make him an help meet for him. Genesis*
> *2:18 (KJV)*

In some versions of the bible, it says a "helper comparable to him." The main idea behind a "helper" is for man and wife to come together to bring out the best in each other. This will allow them to fulfill God's purpose in the marriage and reflect His image upon the earth. My wife has been my biggest cheerleader, and if she had not been in my corner, I would probably be drowning in sorrow. God has used her to be a source of encouragement, and if anyone expects to win in life, they will need this type of support. For married men, your wife should be your support. For married women, your husband should be your support. If you are single, you must surround yourself with Godly friends that will encourage you and those who are not afraid to tell you the truth.

We must learn to appreciate the spouse we have chosen whom God has joined us with. We also should greatly appreciate those caring friends that surround us. There was a time when I did not value my wife. I would often compare her to the wives of other men I knew. I would say things like," Why can't my wife do what so-and-so's wife does?" My wife was pretty much a housewife from the beginning of our marriage. I would often try to impose unrealistic expectations upon her by trying to push her down a career path that did not compliment her talent and gifting. I was more concerned about what I wanted and my image. I did not understand that being a homemaker held just as much value, if not more, than having a prosperous career outside of the home. Though I knew in the back of my mind that my children benefited greatly from my wife being at home. I still viewed the role of a full-time homemaker as being old-fashioned and antiquated. My lack of appreciation for my wife often made her feel like a failure. How do I know this? She would often tell me this with tears running down her face. She yearned for my approval. The bible says the men should dwell with their wives with understanding and to love them like Christ love the church.[7]

Likewise, the bible instructs the wife to submit to her husband out of respect and honor. Not as a doormat or someone to be walked on. She is his equal.[8] I cannot speak from a women's point of view. Still, the bible instructs the men to love their wives and to sacrifice and suffer any discomfort for the sake of the family's wellbeing. I do understand that

---

[7] See 1st Peter 3:7; Ephesians 5:25
[8] See Ephesians 5:22; Colossians 3:18

some of you who are reading this book may not be married and therefore do not have the benefits of a helpmeet from a marital perspective. However, the bible does address the value of good friendships that can provide you with wise Godly counsel. Let's take a look at Jonathan and David. Jonathan often interceded on David's behalf to his father, King Saul, when he sought to do harm to David. The bible says that Jonathan and David loved each other as their own soul, meaning that they considered each other as brothers.[9] Another example of friendships in the bible is Jesus' friends, Lazarus, Mary, and Martha. Jesus often spent time at Lazarus' home. Lazarus and his sisters Mary and Martha regularly attended to the needs of Jesus and His disciples. Now the bible does not go into great detail of the depths of their friendship. Still, it is heavily implied that Jesus was very close friends with Lazarus and his sisters (See John 11: 1-5). I believe that as friends, they shared each other's concerns and probably encouraged one another.

> *As iron sharpens iron, So a man sharpens the countenance of his friend. Proverbs 27:17 (NKJV)*

God created us to be social and relational beings. He never meant for us to dwell in isolation. Behind every successful man and woman, there is someone they have confided in for support. For the married man or woman, they have their spouses. For those who are single, they have their family and friends. No one prospers or attains success on their own. As Proverbs 27:17 implies, we are meant to sharpen each other. Sometimes the words from our "help meet" will cut us. The truth we are told by those who care about us is not meant to wound or gravely injure us but to convict us when we are wrong. These people in our lives will always challenge us to be better and to never settle for anything less than God's best. They will encourage us and not enable us to dwell in self-destructive behavior.

At the beginning of our marriage, my wife struggled with being a helpmeet. Not because of any fault of her own. I drained her so much, and she did not want to hurt me. It wasn't the best approach, and it enabled me to evade responsibility for my own emotional and spiritual

---

[9] See 1 Samuel 18: 1-4

health. But! When my wife had enough, she invoked tough love and became what I needed. I resisted and tried the usual mind tricks, but she said, "These are not the droids you are looking for!" As you can tell, I'm a Star Wars fan. The "force" was dominant in her that day. Even though my wife took her stand, several years went by before she saw the fruit of her labor. During this fight, she still never cursed me or disrespected me but continued to encourage me. She continued to speak life and did not partake in my pity parties. She would remind me that I was the man and king of our household, and I needed to take my rightful place on the throne. Even to this day, if Keshah sees a funk about me (I have a bad attitude). She refuses to entertain anything less than the best from her king and man of God, as she says. When she speaks to me like that, it makes me walk with my back straight and strut like Mufasa from the Lion King. Now, as a result of her being such a beautiful helpmeet, it helped me develop. Listen, gentlemen, women are not like men; what works for us does not work for them. I learned this the hard way. I went to God's Word for answers and help, but even after that, I still botched it up a little. The Word of God says:

> *Husbands, in the same way, live with your wives with an understanding of their weaker nature yet showing them honor as coheirs of the grace of life, so that your prayers will not be hindered. I Peter 3:7 (HCSB)*

Guys, the quickest way to receive unanswered prayers is for you to mistreat your wife. Now, I am not talking about blatantly rude and vile behavior; how God feels about this is obvious. What I am talking about is more subtle. I'm speaking of mishandling your wife. As the verse implies, we must dwell with them with understanding and knowledge. The best way I can describe mishandling one's wife would be akin to using an adjustable wrench to drive a nail into a board as opposed to using a hammer. You may eventually force the nail through the board, probably with damage to the wrench, but the hammer is clearly the proper tool and better choice for the job. This is what it's like when we mistreat our wives. We must gather and use the right tools. We must be gentle and kind. When you think about it, both the husband and wife must use the correct tools and respect one another. As for those of you who are single, everything done for one another must not be done for selfish gain but for the benefit of others. Love and kindness is the best gift to give. As the scripture says, love must be the motivating factor for all of our actions.

I am so thankful that my wife is the type of woman she is. I believe that if I were married to any other woman that did not have my wife's heart, they would have divorced me. I do not condone divorce, except for there is an abuse of any kind (physical, verbal or emotional, etc.). My behavior at the beginning of my marriage was unacceptable and draining. The patience required from my wife would have stretched the limits of any other woman. Husbands, our helpmeets, are designed to help us grow in our manhood. My wife handled this task magnificently. Godly friends should also be able to aid us in becoming better persons, and one day you could return the favor in love. The bible says that it is not good if we are alone. When God made Eve, He didn't just make anyone, He made someone comparable to help Adam in his growth and development. Therefore we must not be prideful and say things like, "What can a woman show me?" A woman can show us, men a great deal. As men, we are charged by God to lead our families in righteousness and be the head of our homes. Our position as the head does not give us permission to rule over our wives, belittle them or treat them as if their opinions don't matter.

To all of the wives that are reading this book, ask God to help you to be the best helpmeet, you can be for your husbands. I know that some of you may be in a hard situation, similar to my wife's position at the beginning of our marriage. I can tell you that I am thankful to God every day that Keshah never gave up on me. I have learned to be a better husband, father, and provider for my family. Each day I feel more successful, like a winner because I am a winner. I will continue to win every day because I serve a victorious God, and I cherish the awesome helpmeet He has blessed me with.

Who can find a virtuous wife? For her worth is far above rubies. The heart of her husband safely trusts her; so he will have no lack of gain. She does him good and not evil all the days of her life. Proverbs 31:10-12 (NKJV)

SEVEN

THE GOOD, THE BAD, BE THANKFUL

But he said to her, "You speak as one of the foolish women speaks. Shall we indeed accept good from God, and shall we not accept adversity?" In all this Job did not sin with his lips. Job 2:10 (NKJV)

As I begin this chapter, I cannot help but reflect upon the lean years my family had experienced in the past. Those times of adversity were filled with many sorrows. Some were the direct consequence of bad choices, while others were just a part of living life in a fallen world. Yet amid that pain, my family and I experienced some of our most cherished memories that solidified our bond. While I am writing this book, I am facing yet another and potentially life-altering situation. After 10 ½ years in the oil and gas industry, I am now unemployed again. Not by choice or any fault of my own, but due to the current state of the economy. Although I have done the best I could to be financially responsible, the long term effects of being without employment could threaten my family's quality of life. We could lose everything. Why do I mention this? Why am I being so transparent about my issues? My reasons are that I do not take lightly the difficulties one will experience in life. I also do not want to bore my readers with a bunch of superficial clichés laden with churchy catchphrases. The issues we face in life are genuine and need real answers. God is aware of our state of affairs and takes no pleasure in our pain, even when we are the cause of our own suffering. God is never caught off guard by our experiences. The Lord says:

> I have told you these things so that in Me you may have peace. You will have suffering in this world. Be courageous! I have conquered the world. John 16:33 (HCSB)

In my time of need, the scriptures are the only thing that has kept me from going off the deep end. When times are good, we also need God's Word to keep us from becoming full of ourselves. When we fall upon hard times, we need to remember God is faithful and will not fail us. The bible tells us that we should be thankful in all things, but I must admit that sometimes this is hard for me to do. I do not think anyone enjoys suffering, whether it's due to our own decisions or life's circumstances. I know that everyone, sooner or later, experiences difficult times. If you're experiencing one now, God will not forsake you. If you are one of those people who have not gone through an experience that will shake you to your core, just keep on living.

When I was new to the faith, the stories I read in the bible were just that, inspirational stories. At times, I found myself gasping in disbelief when I would read passages in the scripture that displayed Israel's rebellion towards God. Especially after He'd deliver them from great peril. I would say to myself, "How could they do that?" As I started walking out my faith and facing my own Red Seas. I found myself wavering in my faith, just like the children of Israel, and doubting God's love for me. Now, as a mature Christian, I have come to understand that what we encounter in life does not alter how God feels about us. And that when bad things happen, this does not mean I am being punished by God. For example, Joseph's story found in the book of Genesis. Joseph was the favored son of Jacob from his beloved wife, Rachel. Joseph was given the finest of everything. Joseph was also endowed with the gift of interpreting dreams by God.

Mostly everyone, whether Christian or not, has heard the story of Joseph. There's even a cartoon movie made about his life that's filled with inspiration and forgiveness. I have tried to imagine from my limited human perspective what he really went through. I wonder about the thoughts he may have had about those who treated him with such cruelty, the fear, the anger and betrayal he must have felt. If I allowed my imagination to paint a picture of what Joseph was experiencing and feeling, I would see a man fighting for every ounce of sanity. Picture if you will, being thrown in a deep dark pit by your own brothers, the brothers that you looked up to for guidance and protection. Imagine these brothers throwing you in a hole, and you're left there for hours screaming for help, not knowing if you were going to live or die. Afterward, they sell you into slavery all because they are jealous of you. You are dragged through the sand, hungry, hair wildly grown out, and probably stinking really bad. Can you imagine what Joseph was thinking? He may have been asking, "What did I do to deserve this? Where is the God of Abraham, Isaac, and my father, Jacob? Maybe I deserve this, maybe it is my fault." Can you feel Josephs's pain?

Days turn into weeks, weeks turn into months, and then the caravan that purchased you from your brothers put you on the auction block in Egypt to be sold again. We assume that Potiphar placed the first bid for Joseph, but I am sure that there were probably other bids for Joseph. The bible just says that the Midianites had sold him into Egypt to Potiphar, an officer of Pharaoh and captain of the guard. It did not say he was the first bidder. God's love placed Joseph in Potiphar's service. The bible also does not give the length of time it took for Joseph to go from being a regular servant to second in control of Potiphar's house. Several years could have went passed. The bible says that God was with Joseph, and he eventually became the top dog next to Potiphar. At this point in Joseph's life, he probably had accepted the fact that he was never going to see his parents or family ever again. After all, even though he perhaps longed to see his family, God was prospering him. What else could go wrong? Well, Joseph finds himself in another unfortunate predicament and is falsely accused of raping Potiphar's wife and ends up spending several of his prime adult years in prison. But, the bible says that God was with him, and even while in prison, he obtained favor.

Now the cartoon and even the movies about Joseph's life do not provide an accurate presentation on the dungeons and prison cells of the ancient world. Several years back, I had the opportunity to visit Gotland

Island in Sweden. While I was there, I toured the ruins of old missions from each era of the conquest of the island. I also had a chance to visit the dungeons from the old castle fort. And let me tell you, they are not as spacious or well-lit (except for the light from the damaged walls) or well-proportioned as the movies depict them to be. They were small and probably overcrowded and filled with the stench of death and dung. There was no comfort. Though the bible says that God was with Joseph and he had favor with the guards, it does not mean he was comfortable. Joseph probably had flashbacks from what his brothers had done to him many years before and perhaps was experiencing PTSD (post-traumatic stress disorder). The story continues with Joseph interpreting the dreams of Pharaohs' butler and baker, only to be forgotten by the butler once the butler was freed, experiencing betrayal again. The bible says that after two full years, Pharaoh started having disturbing dreams that not even his wise men could interpret. It was then that the butler remembered Joseph and his abilities to interpret dreams. Though the bible says, two full years went by before Pharaoh started having those dreams. It did not say that Joseph was immediately summoned by Pharaoh to interpret his dream. More time could have gone by before the chief butler remembered Joseph and his abilities. To make a long story short, we all know how it ended for Joseph as he became the second in command only to Pharaoh. Wow, talk about the experience from the school of hard knocks! When I recap Joseph's story, I find several key things in his life.

1. God was always with him.
2. Everywhere Joseph went, he had favor from those over him.
3. He prospered wherever he was.

The bible never said Joseph doubted God's faithfulness or told that he was not angry or scared. From human experience, we can probably surmise that Joseph probably had a plethora of emotions during his hardships. At times, Joseph's life depicted a stream of nothing but failure and heartache; yet we see the scripture say with each evolution of his life, God was with him. He obtained favor from his masters, and he prospered under every circumstance. I would also like to suggest that during each breakthrough, God was bringing Joseph to a point where he had a thankful heart. Joseph was totally dependent upon God and not himself. You see, God gave Joseph a vision 13 years before his end state. Joseph, like many of us, receive grand ideas but do not consider the conditioning God has to take us through to be equipped for the task. Joseph probably thought that at the time he had these dreams, it was going to happen quickly, and he would be admired as being someone great. I am not saying that Joseph, as a boy, was not thankful or grateful. The Apostle Paul says it like this:

> *When I was a child, I spoke like a child, I thought like a child, I reasoned like a child. When I became a man, I put aside childish things. For now we see indistinctly, as in a mirror, but then face to face. Now I know in part, but then I will know fully, as I am fully known. I Corinthians 13:11-12 (HCSB)*

Joseph was 30 years old when he stood before Pharaoh, but when he left his father's house, he was a 17-year-old boy. Joseph had certainly faced the good, the bad, and the ugly in his life, but was he thankful? Now I am going to stretch this story a bit again because the bible does not give day by day accounts of the emotional state of Joseph while going through. Although the Bible says that God was with him, it does not mean that he did not experience times of sorrow, regret, and anger because of his afflictions. Joseph probably reflected on the lessons that his father had taught him. I could imagine Joseph saying to himself during these lessons, "Why do I need this, and how are these teachings relevant to me now?" Does that sound familiar? I can also imagine him, after having an outburst of anger during his darkest time, calming himself down and reminiscing over the stories his daddy had told him. The stories about how the young Jacob was a trickster, but God taught him humility and how to be a man of integrity. The story about when his father wrestled with the angel of the Lord until God blessed him. Joseph probably used those stories, along with lessons he learned from his father, to develop his prayer life and a heart of gratitude towards God. In turn, God was with him, prospered him, and allowed him to obtain favor with those in authority over him when he was a slave. As Christians, we must have the fruit of thankfulness. To produce this type of fruit, we must have good seed in us to produce good fruit. Bad seeds will produce bad fruit, and frustration will rain down upon us.

I now believe that God prepares us for every trial in advance with some form of training. My Pastor has often mentioned this in her sermons. We must understand that God uses the trials we face and the pain we endure to strengthen us for his service as He did with Joseph. I must admit that before attending my current church home, I thought that bad things, except for sorrow from bad choices, just happened for no reason or purpose at all. I have come to realize that God, like any good trainer, prepares His people. We have to be taught how to trust and depend on God. We need to be taught how to pray and be thankful regardless of what we are going through. When we become new Christians, we experience a heightened sense of joy and excitement. We are so pumped up and excited to be saved that we want to tell everyone, family or foe, about Jesus. It is also common for those that are new to the faith to have a burning desire to preach and give their testimony before the masses, whether large or small. This is not a bad thing, but the problem with this is that as newborn babes, we are not battle-tested. We are not prepared for spiritual battle. We must be taught correct biblical doctrine to sow good seed. God has given my family a Pastor that teaches from her heart and is after God's heart to provide us with His instructions. In Joseph's case, his dad was his teacher.

> *I will give you shepherds who are loyal to Me, and they will shepherd you with knowledge and skill. Jeremiah 3:15 (HSCB)*

God gives us pastors that will instruct us in His ways with sound doctrine. The problem is not that we do not have good teaching, the issue is that the student may refuse to accept or apply the teaching to their lives. Another problem is that some of us have been under instruction that has been laden with evil seeds. God knows what we need to grow and to become mature in His kingdom. We need to have thankful hearts filled with praise and adoration towards our Creator. God does not expect us to like every situation and circumstance we find ourselves in. Still, He does expect us to have a heart of gratitude and thanksgiving.

I know that I have focused mostly on Joseph's story for the vast majority of this chapter to drive home my point. There are other characters in the bible, such as David, Job, Esther, Naomi, Gideon, and many more. I chose Joseph because his story does not share much about the emotional trauma he had experienced during his imprisonment. However, in the end, when he reunites with his family, he is overwhelmed with emotion.

How in the world can someone be thankful for that throughout the entire ordeal? My answer has always been, "Man, I do not know outside of having faith in God." All I do know is that when you come before God with a thankful heart full of praise, He moves. When I was seemingly facing some of the worst times of my life, and even now, as I am writing this chapter, God shows up when I praise and thank Him. You see, those feel-good scriptures that we Christians quote in piety did not come alive for me until I came up against life's brick wall. Does God know that we are in pain? Yes, He does! Does God know that we may be on our last leg? Yes, He does! But, I have learned that God does not move when we complain, even if we may have a good reason to do so. The bible says to:

> *Enter His gates with thanksgiving and His courts with praise. Give thanks to Him and praise His name. Psalm 100:4 (HCSB)*

We do not enter in with complaints and accusations, but with praise and a heart of thanksgiving. I know it is easier said than done; trust me, I know. Remember, at the end of chapter 6, when I explained how God moved on behalf of my family? Man, we were in bad shape. My mind was at a point of saying to my wife and children, "Let's consume what we have left; for tomorrow, we perish." No, I was not thinking of physically harming myself or my family. Still, in my mind, we seemingly had nothing to look forward to. I'm so glad that I lifted up my voice to the Lord, thanked Him, and gave Him praise and watched Him move immediately. At that moment, I knew that God truly inhabited the praise of His people. Now I understand why the psalmist could say:

> *I will praise the Lord at all times; His praise will always be on my lips. I will boast in the Lord; the humble will hear and be glad. Psalm 34:1-2 (HCSB)*

Also, when he says:

> *So I will praise You as long as I live; at Your name, I will lift up my hands. You satisfy me as with rich food; my mouth will praise You with joyful lips. Psalm 63:4-5 (HCSB)*

I must apologize because, at the beginning of this book, I said I will hold back from using a lot of the "catchy Christian lingo," but I can't help but to. To me, these scriptures that magnify God in praise and adoration are much more than catchphrases of Christian piety. They are life, they are bread, they are my medicine, they are my counsel, instruction, and they are my hope. They are embedded into everything that I am. When I begin to smell the funk of life rising up into my nostrils, I lift up my hands with thanksgiving and praise. When I experience great success, I praise God. When my employer cut my hours at work, I give God praise and thank Him for the increase. When my coworkers talk about me, I remember that I am not worthless but fearfully and wonderfully made. I have learned that we must continually offer up the sacrifice of praise to God, that is, the fruit of our lips, giving thanks to His name.

If we pick back up on Joseph's story after he became second in command only to Pharaoh, he once again encounters his brothers during Egypt's famine. Joseph's brothers did not recognize him. Yet, I can only imagine what he must have been feeling. The bible does give us a glimpse of the possible emotions Joseph was most likely experiencing. When he saw his brothers, he had put them through several tests to see whether or not they were the same heartless individuals who sold him into slavery. To make a long story short, Joseph finally reveals himself to his brothers making for an emotional family reunion. What I have learned is that God uses the problems we face in life to prepare us for greater works. Whether the issues are a result of our own bad choices or, in Joseph's case, no fault of our own, God wants to use them to elevate us for His purpose and glory.

Pretty much my whole tenure at the oil and gas company appeared to be a complete failure. It seemed like I could not do anything right. I became the guy no one wanted on their team for kickball. I found myself doubting whether or not I made the right choice to leave my previous employer, a company that I had prospered at for several years. However, the challenges I had experienced at my new job caused me to fall on my knees and do some deep introspective thinking. I started offering up praises to God and thanking Him for greater things. I also started reading the bible more. I began to invest my time in reading books from Christian authors and some of the best thinkers from the past and present century. Of course, the bible is my primary source for receiving instruction from God. Still, I also found that it pays high dividends by expanding my knowledge through excellent teachers God has placed on this earth. I have made it my chief aim to be thankful at all times and offer up a sacrifice of praise to God even when it appears nothing is going to change.

Since 2015, I made it a practice before I start my day to pray and write down three things I'm thankful for. I know there should be more than three things, and there is, but I focus on three. Then at the end of my day, I find one good thing that happens during my day, whether big or small and write it down. What I am doing is keeping a track record of God's goodness so that I can reflect upon them occasionally. Reader, whatever way you choose, let it be tempered by the truth of God's word. Let me be clear, God will get the glory. I believe God rewards those who come before Him with a thankful heart full of praise and adoration. I cannot say this enough.

EIGHT

I AM WELL ABLE BECAUSE
I SEE GREATER

*Then Caleb quieted the people in the presence of Moses
and said, "We must go up and take possession of the
land because we can certainly conquer it! Numbers 13:30
(HCSB)*

have found that it is easy to believe a task or goal is achievable when
there is an abundance of resources available to complete the objective.
Even in my own life, I have a tendency to go for it when conditions
appear to be favorable to win. I have also learned that when we walk
with God, He allows us to come up against situations that are impossible
for us to accomplish on our own. In light of this, many of us have
resided to stay in our comfort zones. We stay there because we are
comfortable, and everything appears to be stable. For instance, if I
had known ahead of time what I would have to face with my previous
employer, I probably would have stayed with the other company. I had
a stable salary, though it barely met my family's needs. I was good at
what I did, even though I was bored and unchallenged, and I was able
to see my family every day. I had all of the ingredients for stagnation
in the name of comfort and stability, so when the offer came to work
for an oil and gas company, I took the challenge. Little did I know that
the problems I would encounter would be dealing with the unfavorable
personalities associated with working offshore. Not everyone offshore
is difficult to work with. Still, offshore life is not a work environment

for thin-skinned and faint-hearted individuals. When I asked God for a challenge, I was thinking technical, but God had something else in mind. Let me tell you, what I experienced was thus far one of the most challenging yet rewarding times in my life. During that time, I have learned to call upon and depend upon God like never before. I learned to be thankful at all times, developed tough skin, and grew stronger to fight against the enemy.

Do not get me wrong; both of these employers are excellent companies, but like any company, they are subject to the changes in our global economy. In my case, I was just one of the many casualties from the changing oil and gas industry. What does this have to do with being well able or seeing greater? I am glad you asked. It has everything to do with it. My experience is not unique to me. Everyone will eventually face in life the decision to grow under pressure or die in complacency. Either we will rise to the occasion and see an opportunity or die from misfortune. It really depends upon our perspective on how we view the things we face. God knows this is a difficult concept for us to grasp. I wrestled with this for a very long time. If anyone tells you this is easy to do, I would beg to differ. We all must learn to see the greater and believe we can do all things through Christ. We also must be careful that we are operating out of biblical truth as opposed to dwelling in the spooky "name it and claim it" realm. For example, if someone tells you to participate in a Jericho march around a home that your current income cannot afford. This is neither biblical nor an act of faith; it is an unrealistic and rather stupid jester.

About 5 years into my marriage, I was laid off from my employer in Austin, which I have mentioned earlier in this book. We found ourselves facing pretty much the same thing we are facing today, going through our savings while looking for work to make ends meet. The bills were piling up, and we had no money left except for our car payment. We were also attending a church that spent just as much time on tithe and offering as they did on praise & worship, which was very long. Well, one Wednesday night service, I decided to step out on faith and gave our entire car note in the offering. We had already given our tithe & offering from my last check, but I was desperate. The preacher was so compelling. That I believed that if I gave my car payment, somehow,

God would miraculously pay off our car and bring abundance in our life. On the surface, this would look like a genuine act of faith. And in many of those spooky environments, we would be applauded. I told my wife what I had done, and she nearly collapsed. Needless to say, I had to hear a lot of crying on the way home from the Chevrolet dealership while all five of us were crammed into my wife's grandfather 1991 Ford Escort hatchback. Now, you think that I would have learned my lesson from this experience, but I did not. Several months had passed, and I did the same boneheaded thing, but this time there was no money involved because there was no money. I had convinced myself and my wife to catch a bus to a car dealership and tell them that God said to give us a car. When we made it to the dealership, the salesman showed us different models, and when we found the one we wanted, I told him that God said to give us that car. With a straight face, the car salesman replied, "Did God give you a down payment?" Once again, I had to look into my wife's confused, crying eyes. My wife and I laugh about these stories now, but back then, they were no laughing matter. Sad to say, many of us have experienced this type of misappropriation of true faith. Too many times, we only think of ourselves or obtaining material gain when we think of accomplishing more significant things for God.

Let's look at the prayer of Jabez. There was a time when this prayer was misused by many Christians as a magical formula that could help them obtain wealth and influence. However, a more in-depth look at the request of Jabez was not about personal gain, but about a man who wanted to be useful in the hands of God. Instead of being a burden, Jabez wanted to be a blessing to others. This should be our motive when it comes to achieving any form of greatness; we need to have others and generations on our minds. We must be generational-minded because our impact on life will be felt by future generations. It is crucial that what we leave behind reflects the glory of God and not death & destruction. There are several things we must be aware of if we are ever to reach our God-given potential and achieve greatness:

- Wickedness must not be an option in our life.
- A crisis is not synonymous with defeat.
- Failure in life is not the product of a lack of potential.

- Whether we fail or succeed, win or lose in life does not depend on God but on us.
- Anything we refuse to use to glorify God, the devil will pervert and direct for his use.

One of the problems I believe that plagues mankind, especially the church, is the lack of appreciation for the talents that we possess. Each one of us is uniquely created by God to achieve a particular purpose and goal in life. However, if we are ignorant of our potential and or show a lack of appreciation for how God created us. We will tend to star gaze upon someone else's gifts and try to mimic them or become envious. As with the above bullets, we will misuse what God has put in us and put the blame on someone or something else other than ourselves.

When opportunity knocks, it is never without a challenge. What I have come to learn is that it is not the object of the opportunity that God is focused on, but it is the stored potential He wants to release out of us; that's the real prize. God is so gracious that He doesn't just give it to us all at once. He takes us through various regiments of conditioning to build us up for greater challenges and victories. Think about when David chose to face off against Goliath. Before this encounter, God had already put David through the necessary training to accomplish the task. What if David had rebelled and complained to his father about keeping the sheep? He would have never received the conditioning for defeating Goliath, let alone the confidence to even face him. There are no shortcuts to achieving greatness, and the following are essential to achieving it:

1. Belief
2. Sacrifice
3. Focus and fight to stay focused
4. Hard work
5. The ability to say "no."
6. Greatness is in you

If we first do not believe we can achieve greatness through the power of God or waver back and forth, we can go no further. We are done. The bible calls this type of person unstable and double-minded. This type of person should not expect to receive anything from God. I was like this for a long time. I would pray and doubt then get upset with God because my conditions were not changing. There must also be a sacrifice to be able to achieve greatness. I used to have the mindset of wanting something for nothing. I attributed miracles from God as merely asking Him for something then, abracadabra, it was supposed to magically appear or happen. Although there are many miracles performed in the bible, most of what I was asking God for was materialistic and did not require a miracle to obtain it. All I needed was the discipline to sacrifice and not indulge in short term pleasures for the long term goal. I believe that we need to give God something to work with. God knows what is in us, and He is not going to force us to give it to Him. We have to give it freely so that God can yield an increase with it. In the book of Exodus, God asked Moses what was in his hand. Moses replied, "a rod," and God worked miracles through Moses with that rod. Also, in II Kings 4, a widow approached Elisha about petitioning God on her behalf over the debt her dead husband had left her. Elisha asked her what did she have in her house, and she replied, "A small jar of olive oil." Elisha gave her instructions from God to follow, and what she had in her possession increased. All we have to do is give God something He can work with and believe He will maximize it, and we will see the increase. I am not talking about a halfhearted effort. We have to present something of quality, intention, and focus. Being able to focus and becoming greater goes conjointly with one's ability to believe that what they are going after is achievable. If you believe something, you will be focused on accomplishing whatever it takes for it to come to pass. If you are focused on reaching your goal, then you'll believe it can be done despite it being painful. Let's not forget hard work and the ability to say no to all distractions. When I started seeking a deeper commitment to God and His purpose for my life, I had resolved to put forth maximum effort for the journey. I call it a journey because seeking God is never-ending, and it just gets better with time. Anyhow, I had placed some restrictions upon what I would allow myself to think, say, watch, and do. This is about the time I had resolved to write down three things I was thankful for before starting my workday and finding something good to write down by the end of the day. I had to be very intentional. My flesh did not want to cooperate with getting up 1 to 2 hours before the time for me to get ready for work, pray, read the bible, and write in my journal. I also committed to keeping myself in physical shape, reading books to help develop my mind and writing in my journal. I worked 12 hour days but was averaging 5 to 6 hours of sleep out of a 24-hour cycle. In the beginning, I was so tired, but I was determined to stay the course, work hard, and say no to the distraction of sleep, TV, and the internet. To me, there was a lot at stake, and my mind needed a lot of work. Had I not stayed the course and believed God for a mental breakthrough. There is no way I could have kept my sanity while enduring the stress of working offshore and being away from my family. Lastly, we must know that there is greatness on the inside of us. If Christ, the hope of glory dwells in those of us that are born again. Then we have greatness in us already; we just have to fall in line with the Holy Spirit so that all of that God-given potential can be released. As the bible says:

I can do all things through Christ who strengthens me.
Philippians 4:13 (NKJV)

When I reflect upon the title of this book, "I Choose to Win," and the current chapter, "I Am Well Able Because I See Greater." I do understand that many of you reading this book are facing severe challenges. You need more than just another motivational speech. I completely understand. Your situation may be causing you great pain, but rising above, it has the potential to change everything. Be encouraged; that unknown change could push you to greatness. We fear change can also cause long-term suffering. Even in this, we must not be stifled by fear but be prayerful and trust God.

I opened up this chapter with an excerpt out of the book of Numbers 13:30. The 12 spies had just returned from their mission and had given their report. Except for Joshua and Caleb, the other spies, gave bad news, which made all of the Israelites scared and afraid. All of the spies agreed that the land God had told them to take was just what He promised it would be, and they even brought back the proof. However, ten of the spies focused on what appeared to be bad (the challenges), and Caleb tried to calm them down. It would be tempting to judge the children of Israel for being afraid, especially after God has continuously shown them His power through many signs and wonders. But before we do, stop and think about our own lives. How many times has God performed great things for us only to see us quake in fear when a more challenging issue or event arises? I do not believe the fear part is the issue, I think it is how we respond to the fear. There can be a healthy fear because the bible tells us to fear God. There are many references in the Scripture regarding fearing God from a healthy perspective. We do not walk around terrified of Him; however, as a Christian, we need to understand that He has the power to give and take life (See Matthew 10:8). Everyone has a bit of reservation when faced with a task that seems more significant than what we are. But, as my current Pastor points out, God prepares us for the test before we face it, not when we encounter it. The problem is that most of us do not follow the training required to be prepared for these events.

When my family and I were living in Minnesota, God was blessing us tremendously, even though the initial move was filled with difficulties. God had placed us in a wonderful church and surrounded us with many wonderful mentors like Ray & Mom Sue Christian, Ben & Ruth Lee, Bob Bayer & family, Pastor Gordy, and many others. My employer wanted to train me to become an engineer. God was basically spoon-feeding my opportunity, but I could not see it or instead refused to see it. I was so preoccupied with getting back to Texas and away from Minnesota's cold weather & high taxes. I wanted to return to what was familiar, be around family, old friends, and chase the dollar. I believe that eventually, my family and I were going to return back to Austin, Texas. Still, God was trying to work character flaws out of me first. He was doing so many wonderful things for my family that some of them could qualify as biblical type miracles. Unfortunately, I viewed God's wonderful works from a "takers" mentality. Instead of drawing close to seek God's heart, I stayed on the superficial level and continued to seek His hand only.

As I mentioned, back in the year 2000, I took the job with a company in Austin that appeared to be filled with so much promise and moved my family back to Austin, Texas. It was a disastrous move. I lasted one year before being laid off. I had started a cycle that put my family in a spiritual and financial wilderness for seven years. Just like the children of Israel, I did not pay attention to the training. God was grooming Israel for greatness. He took them the hard way to teach them how to fight and how to be tough. When they had reached their limits, He showed them that He would fight for them. This is what God was trying to do with me, but I did not pay attention to it. Despite the miracles and mentors, I chose not to listen to God's wisdom, and when I came face to face with adversity, I buckled. It almost cost me my life and my marriage. I found myself saying, "I am not able to go up against this." Is this where you are right now? Are you paralyzed by fear such that it eclipses the power of God and His faithfulness He has shown you many times over? REMEMBER YOUR TRAINING SOLDIER! We are more than conquers in Christ Jesus. Yes, we may get cut, scars are cool, God is good, and in Christ, we have the victory. I see greater; I want greater, and I am well able to do it!

N I N E

SPEAK THE WORD, AND BELIEVE

"Lord," the centurion replied, "I am not worthy to have You come under my roof. But only say the word, and my servant will be cured." Matthew 8:8 (HCSB)

We live in a time that has a fixation on instant gratification. Everyone seems to want to be in a hurry to obtain bigger and better of everything. New technology becomes almost obsolete as soon as it is released. And relationships? Well, don't get me started on that. Patience has truly become a lost virtue, and I must admit that at times it had been a missing virtue in my own life. I have come to realize that trying to make things happen due to impatience leads to potentially disastrous results. Have you ever said, "If I knew then what I know now I would have…." you know the rest. The truth is we probably wouldn't have done anything differently if our hearts and wills were not in sync with God's timing. This is obvious, especially if we keep repeating the same mistakes. Remember the quote, "a lesson not learned will and must be repeated." In the scripture, a Roman Centurion approaches Jesus and asks Him to heal a sick servant of his. Jesus was ready to come to the Centurions aid. The Centurion told Jesus that he is not worthy of Him to come to his house, but just speak the Word, and his servant will be healed. The Centurion understood Jesus' authority. Because the Centurion understood this, he was able to believe Jesus at His Word. He knew that whatever Jesus said, would be done. We must be like the

Centurion when it comes to believing God's Word. Although it was Jesus who spoke the Word to heal the Centurions servant, the Centurion had unwavering faith in God. God gives us the authority to speak His word not only over our lives but others as well. The bible says:

Now without faith it is impossible to please God, for the one who draws near to Him must believe that He exists and rewards those who seek Him. Hebrews 11:6 (HCSB

We must:

- Have faith in God
- Believe God
- Seek God

The Centurion respected the Jewish community and humbled himself from his position and acknowledged the authority of the God of the Jews. Roman Centurions were high ranking officers. If he wanted to exert his power to get to Jesus, it would have been very little the Jewish community could do about it. However, he chose to humble himself out of respect for their God and His people. We also must humble ourselves before God if we are to expect anything from Him.

Sadly in modern-day Christianity, speaking God's Word over one's life has been reduced to a plea to God for wealth, power, and good health. Although having these things are not wrong, our motives behind most of these requests are purely selfish and have nothing to do with advancing the kingdom of God. I am not saying that poverty is synonymous with holiness because this is not true. Poor people can be overcome with greed and the preoccupation of material things just like anyone else. Sin is universal and non-discriminatory when it comes to mankind. God wants us to prosper materially and spiritually. God has given us His creative power as His children when we obey Him and speak His Word. We cannot reduce this power down to the acquisition of bread (material wants, needs, control, etc.) for our personal gain. God is not mocked. He knows our agenda. He knows whether we are seeking His will or His hand. Jesus had sharp words for the people who were just seeking Him for his hand only. He knew the difference between someone genuinely seeking to believe and do His will from those who just wanted the goods he provided (miracles, etc.). Jesus said:

> *I assure you: You are looking for Me, not because you saw the signs, but because you ate the loaves and were filled. Don't work for the food that perishes but for the food that lasts for eternal life, which the Son of Man will give you, because God the Father has set His seal of approval on Him. John 6:26-27 (HCSB)*

Years ago, when my wife and I lived in Irving, Texas, we would often play the lottery. We were still newlyweds, and like many young couples, we didn't have much money. We were believers and attended church regularly, but we had a grave misunderstanding regarding speaking God's Word over our lives. We would buy lottery tickets and pray to God to let us hit the right numbers. In our prayers, we would tell God of all the good we would do for the kingdom and how we would be good stewards over the earnings, including paying the tithe. My wife would even start speaking in tongues and thanked God for the harvest. Right after that, we would get into an argument over how much we would give our respective family members. This was so pathetic. I assure you this is a true story. Some of you may be laughing. However, this is an example of how we, as Christians, can be so far from the truth of God's Word and warped in our thinking.

When we speak God's Word over our lives, it transcends our own personal needs and wants. We should be thinking globally. In the book of Acts, Paul and Silas were arrested, beaten, and placed in jail for ministering the Gospel. I am sure both of them did not appreciate their circumstances. Still, instead of complaining to God or even asking Him to get them out of there, the bible says they started singing songs and praising God. Now get this, the bible also said that the guards and the other prisoners heard them. Their praise was so powerful that God caused all of the jail doors to open. Not just Paul and Silas jail cell only. Any of the prisoners could have walked out of their cells and gone free. It was customary during that time for a guard to kill themselves if a prisoner had escaped under their watch. Still, Paul called out to the guard not to harm himself because all of the prisoners were accounted for. This event allowed for the guard and all of the prisoners to witness the power of God. (See Acts 16:25-29) Paul and Silas could have just walked out of the cell and went free, but they chose to stay and seize the opportunity to minister God's Word to the guard and his entire family. Their worship not only set them free, but the guard and his whole family were set free as well. Just imagine if Paul and Silas would have complained and murmured. The guards and the prisoners would have heard that too, and there could have been a very different outcome.

Someone is always watching us, especially if we claim to have faith in Jesus. While working in Minnesota, I shared a cubicle with a man who said he was a Christian. He was one of the most judgmental individuals I have ever met. That summer, a young lady from college was interning there and sat a couple of cubicles down from me. I never had many conversations with her other than "hello" and "goodbye." Well, when the summer had ended, and her internship was over, I found an envelope on my computer keyboard. I opened the envelope, and in it was a letter from the young lady thanking me for being a great example to her in regards to modeling Christ and Godly behavior. I do not remember her words exactly, but she implied that it helped strengthen her faith and commitment to God. She explained that she had witnessed the assaults and attacks on my faith from the other gentlemen claiming to be a Christian. She observed how I never stooped to his level and was always courteous and polite. This young woman was struggling with her faith, even though she grew up in a loving Christian home. She told me that my example helped her to see that it was possible to live a Christian life in the workplace, and she committed her life back to Christ. I neither heard from nor saw this young lady again. As I stated before, you never know who is watching. During that time in my life, I was seeking God to help me to walk upright before Him and not to be overly concerned about my issues. I wanted to be a blessing to others. Her letter blessed me more than any amount of money I could have received. I knew God was answering my prayers because I was able to help someone else. My prayers, speaking God's Word, and believing in Him gave me that extra boost I needed to increase my faith.

Everything that we do has some sort of impact, whether good or bad. What we think about ourselves dictates how we speak and ultimately guide our actions. There is no 'hocus pocus' here, this is a real thing. How we think and what we think about determines the course of our lives. When Jesus reprimanded the Pharisees for their hypocrisy, He tells them:

> Brood of vipers! How can you speak good things when you are evil? For the mouth speaks from the overflow of the heart. Mathew 12:34 (HCSB)

What we say will reveal what we really believe. I've heard it said, and I do believe this. If you want to know how a person thinks, listen to what they are saying or talking about. Believing something takes place in the mind, not our feelings. If believing were about our feelings, then Jesus might have started every statement he says about believing with "If you feel this is true then......." But He did not because He knows that our feelings change and are fickle. Imagine if the writer of Hebrews would have said, "He who comes to God must feel He is..." I don't know about you, but sometimes I may feel like God isn't there, but it's in those times I must believe God despite how I feel. Hebrews, chapter 11, also highlights the faith of our matriarchs. When we trust God, faith is developed. If we do not have faith that God will take care of us and help us, it is impossible to please Him. If we do not have faith, then we will doubt and waver in our commitment to God. If we wrestle with God's ability to answer our prayers, the bible says that we should not expect anything from God. This is because we don't expect anything from God. If we approach God in this manner, then speaking His Word over our lives is reduced to wishful thinking with no expected outcome. If we have no expected result, we will be overtaken by hopelessness.

Similarly, if we say that we believe and have faith in God, then there will be works to back up what we say. During the summer of 2015, my family was at a crossroads with our living conditions. We were staying with friends from church until our home was finished being built. We ended up having to back out of the deal due to major delays from the homebuilder and lost $2500. The end of summer vacation was near, and my children needed to be registered in school. We did not have proof of residency to be able to enroll them in the school district that our friends' neighborhood belonged to. On top of that, their daughter was returning home and needed the room we were occupying.

We ended up finding a new builder who had a home ready to move into, and initially, the deal appeared to be going smooth with no issues. We put everything we had left down on the new home. When we came close to closing, the loan officer told me that we needed to bring $3000 to closing. We did not have $3000, and, on top of that, what we did have was for our tithes. I told my wife that we may have to lose some of what we put down again and wait on buying a home because we were going to honor God first with the tithe and offerings. My wife was disappointed, not because of paying the tithe, but because we were going to lose money again; she was worn out over the whole process. The next day, the loan officer called me back and said that he had made a mistake and that we did not have to bring anything to closing and that we were getting $2450 back. God is so awesome! He restored the money we lost from the first deal.

After reading this, some may think that getting the money back, and being able to get into our home was the blessing. I would like to say that though this was wonderful, the real benefit was seeing how God moves on behalf of those who trust and believe in Him. By faith, we paid our tithe because the tithe belongs to Him. I didn't pay it expecting anything in return. I stood on the word of God and believed what He says in the scriptures:

> *Bring the full tenth into the storehouse so that there may be food in My house. Test Me in this way," says the Lord of Hosts. "See if I will not open the floodgates of heaven and pour out a blessing for you without measure. I will rebuke the devourer for you, so that it will not ruin the produce of your land and your vine in your field will not fail to produce fruit," says the Lord of Hosts. "Then all the nations will consider you fortunate, for you will be a delightful land," says the Lord of Hosts. Malachi 3:10-12 (HCSB)*

Even if we had to lose the home, we'd pay the tithe and give an offering. Why? Because honoring God first is what we do faithfully. The enemy tried to get me to do the opposite and said to me, "Hey, just pay it the next time. God will understand." I believed and trusted God, not the enemy. I spoke God's Word over my family. He saw our situation, and He did not let the enemy interfere. Friends, if we ever expect to win in life, we must trust and believe God. We must not doubt Him. He knows that as human beings, we struggle with this. That's why Jesus came down and dwelt among us so He can identify with our struggles. The scripture says,

> *For we do not have a High Priest who is unable to sympathize with our weaknesses, but One who has been tested in every way as we are, yet without sin. Hebrews. 4:15 (HCSB)*

God is good on His Word. Had I not believed God and held on to the tithe, I probably would have gotten into the home. People buy houses every day, but because my wife and I trusted in God, we contributed to His storehouse so that His work would be done on the earth. I believe others would be touched by our faithfulness to God. Trust in God, speak His word over your lives, believe it, and watch God move.

TEN

IT'S NOT OVER, IT'S TIME TO WIN!

I would have lost heart, unless I had believed that I would see the goodness of the Lord In the land of the living. Wait on the Lord; Be of good courage, And He shall strengthen your heart; Wait, I say, on the Lord! Psalms 27:13-14 (NKJV)

Proclaim this among the nations: Prepare for holy war; rouse the warriors; let all the men of war advance and attack! Joel 3:9 (HCSB)

In the summer of 2016, my youngest son, Joshua, started having problems controlling his anger and showing hostility toward his brother and sister. On one of those episodes, it had gotten so bad that I had to wrestle him down to the ground to get him to calm down. As I held him down, I'll never forget what he said to me. Joshua looked at me with tears running down his face and said, "Dad, I do not want to fail, I want to be successful; I feel like such a failure." I just held him in my arms as I was crying too. I told him that he was not a failure and that he has only just begun his life. I further said to him that God has a good plan for his life, and it is far from being over. Right then, I knew more than anything that the battle we are in against the father of lies, satan, was very much real. Satan will stop at nothing to destroy us, even if it means attacking our children before they have a chance to get started in life.

If I could be honest, I must admit that sometimes I become very concerned about how my life is going at times. I know this may not be a very spiritual thing to say, but it is the truth. I do my best not to dwell on the mistakes and choices I have made in the past. As much as I hate to admit, there are consequences tied to every decision we make, whether good or bad. Even though God forgives us of our sins and does not hold them against us, we still must answer for our actions through the built-in consequence attached to them. For example. If I steal and get arrested, then afterward, I realize that what I have done was wrong, and I ask God for forgiveness. God will forgive me. That does not mean I am off the hook from the consequence. Dealing with the consequences does not mean life is over and that there is no recovery. For instance, King David committed murder to cover up an act of adultery he had committed with Uriah's wife, one of his officers.[10] When God sent Nathan the prophet to confront David about his sins, David repented. David was genuinely sorry for his actions, and God forgave him. However, there were inescapable consequences attached to what he had done. Yet, the bible still refers to him as a "man after God's own heart." I am in no way advocating for or justifying willful acts of sin.

Just like King David, many of us have made dire mistakes with lasting consequences, but that does not mean that God does not love us and cannot use us. Sometimes disappointment hits us at no fault of our own, such as a sickness, a layoff, or even a natural disaster. The damage left behind could seem impossible to recover from. We must remember Job. Job was a righteous man who served God faithfully. God had allowed Job to suffer at the hands of satan. He lost everything except for his life. Job's suffering was so bad that his friends were sure that Job had sinned against God. Job's wife told him to curse God and die; now, that's pretty bad. Then when Job was reaching a breaking point, God had to remind Job that He was the God of the universe and that nothing catches Him by surprise. In the end, God had restored to Job over and above what he had lost.

When tragedy hits, whether due to our own actions like King David or of no consequence of our own like Job, it is easy to take the path

---

[10] See 2nd Samuel 11 Nathan, the prophet, confronts David about Uriah's murder to cover up his adulterous affair with Uriah's wife Bathsheba.

of least resistance and quit. When we deliberately decide to quit, the enemy comes in for the kill and does not let up. He wants to make sure we become utterly ineffective in life and never rise again. This is a terrifying place to be because we become very unstable and susceptible to the following:

- Fear
- Doubt
- Condemnation
- Shame

Being in this place in your mind is like you're drowning. You can't breathe, but you're not dying. God has big plans for our lives, and this was His intentions for mankind when He created us. If God was done with us, He would not have sent His only Son to die for our sins. I have heard it said that none of us came here to be mediocre; bound by the trivial; silenced by hardships and enslaved by the petty. When I was going through my wilderness experience, I was sure that God was done with me. I was overcome with so much guilt from walking in unbelief that I could not see the greatness God had put in me. I had to reach a point where I had to draw a line in the sand and say NO MORE! I needed to make a decision to trust God no matter what, stop settling for mediocrity and start living a victorious life in Christ. I had to stop being concerned about what I did not have and be thankful for what I did have. I had to stop comparing myself to the world's standards but by God's. I had to come to the conclusion that it was not all about me, my family, and my needs; there was clearly a bigger picture, and I had to get in tune with it.

God wants us to be fruitful in every area of our lives. We cannot be productive if we think negatively of ourselves. How we see ourselves affects everything that we do or don't do. We must see ourselves from God's perspective, but if we do not, we will live ineffective lives. The scripture says:

> *Guard your heart above all else, for it is the source of life.*
> *Proverbs 4:23 (HCSB)*

I believe this scripture is referring to keeping our minds so free from toxic thoughts that the decisions we make will be wise and guided by God. I have personally found this to be true in my own life (past and present). When my thoughts were full of doubt and unbelief, my decisions reflected it. When I started depending on God and allowed my thoughts to get in line with what God says about me, my choices and actions revealed that as well. I became very intentional about learning how to see myself the way God did because I was tired of losing in life. I had to realize that to start winning from God's perspective, I had to drop the American dream and get a "God dream." I had to dream beyond worldly success with all of its temporary perks and look at how God wanted to use my life to affect generations to come. When I decided to come out of the wilderness, God started taking me through a process specifically designed for me to become a fruitful person. God began to help me to develop some key attributes I needed to become a winner. God's methods are the same, but His plans and means of bringing us to full maturity and fruitfulness are custom made for us individually. God's plan for me involved developing:

- Godly character
- Tough skin and strength
- Persistence
- Thankfulness and praise

GODLY CHARACTER

As I said, the very first thing God started with was building my character. I had to learn to see things from His perspective, or I would perish. My belief system had to change. Though I've been a professing Christian for years, my faith in God lacked depth. I had no proof to back up what I was professing. My life had no positive impact on the people around me, even my family. You see, what we genuinely believe shapes our character, which translates into our decisions and actions. Basically, we do what we "Believe." I had to work really hard in this area and still do. My first inclination tends to lean towards the negative when faced with challenges, whether big or small. I'm grateful I stopped handling the bible like some science fiction storybook and started disciplining myself to view it as my source of life.

I started asking God to help me to be useful in His hands and to be a blessing to others. The scriptures say that Christians are the "salt of the earth." I did not feel like it, nor did my life reflect it. I desperately wanted to be the Lord's salt, so in addition to praying for my family. I started praying for my coworkers, neighbors, the leaders of our country, people in other countries, and the poor. I started seeking God's heart instead of His hand, speaking life, and speaking His Word in every situation. When I took the focus off of me, my relationship with God was set ablaze. I became more thankful and appreciative of God's grace in my life. God started revealing to me the things that were dear to Him. I started seeing people the way God did, and it helped me to remove the "us and them" religious piety mentality. God loves His creation, even when we misbehave. He wants us that are called by His name to be His hands, feet, and voice in this fallen world. That is why our belief system, which shapes our character, is essential if we are to be fruitful in the things of God. We cannot afford to be depressed and view ourselves as insignificant. By doing this, we significantly devalue the apex of God's creation, us, and His life-transforming power. We cannot be what we do not believe, no matter how much we confess it with our mouths. What we say must be backed up by action that is tempered by Godly motivation. We must believe that we are God's craftsmanship and that we are wonderfully made. We were created to do marvelous works for the kingdom while we are here.

TOUGH SKIN & STRENGTH

The next attribute God started working in me was developing thick skin and persistence. When I left the Marine Corps in 1992, I had allowed myself to develop an inability to stay a steady course when challenged or under pressure. Before I knew it, I found myself living a powerless life. I would start well, but as soon as I was faced with a challenge, I would quit and give up. This time, instead of fighting God, I allowed Him to work His will in my life, even if it was not pleasant. I was determined not to repeat this test again. Since God does not change, He allowed me to face similar obstacles that tripped me up in the past. Once again, I found myself working with challenging personalities and dealing with potentially life-altering circumstances. As I mentioned back in chapter 8, I faced tremendous opposition from Satan at my previous employer in Houston and during my tenure working offshore. I personally do not hold any hostility toward the individuals that intentionally and unintentionally gave me a hard time. Because I know that everything I went through God had allowed it to strengthen me for His work. This world holds no punches, and if we are not able to take a hit every now and then, our sphere of influence would be small.

If you faint in the day of adversity, Your strength is small. Proverbs 24:10 (NKJV)

We can speak a good game, but those around us know what's really happening. I have learned that God will allow us to repeat the same test until we pass it. God wants us to endure hardship, and the only way to learn to endure hardship is by experiencing hardship. I am not talking about suffering issues due to willful sinful behavior. I am talking about issues that are outside of our control. Now in the world of sports, athletes work out to get faster and stronger to become better at what they do. Their workouts are not designed to keep them comfortable; they are designed to squeeze every ounce of peak performance out of the athlete through pain and persistence. If athletes compete for an earthly crown, go through so much pain to obtain a prize that will fade away, what makes those of us who call ourselves Christians think that God would not require us to do the same thing for His kingdom? God is the ultimate life coach because He is the author of life, and He knows the type of training we need to be fully equipped to do His work. God sees us based upon the potential He has placed in us. He allows us to go through what we refer to as hardships to usher us into our rightful role. For example, in the book of Exodus, God calls the children of Israel His army. Israel has been in bondage to Egypt for over 400 years, working as slaves.[11] They had no military training, and rebelling against their oppressors was nowhere on their minds. They hated their position in life, probably felt helpless, and certainly did not see themselves as an army. But, God saw them differently. They needed to be trained to think and see themselves as God did. God took them by way of the wilderness, which was the seemingly hard way. Why? The bible says the following:

> *When Pharaoh let the people go, God did not lead them along the road to the land of the Philistines, even though it was nearby; for God said, "The people will change their minds and return to Egypt if they face war." So He led the people around toward the Red Sea along the road of the wilderness. And the Israelites left the land of Egypt in battle formation. Exodus 13:17-18 (HCSB)*

What I noticed in these scriptures was that the shortest route to the Promised Land was through hostile territory. Although God saw them as His army, He knew that they would faint at the sight of battle without being trained to fight. God decided to take them the "Long Way" to strengthen them. Yes, God could have wiped the hostiles out single-handedly. Still, He wanted to develop and train His people to be warriors and worshipers. Just like with the children of Israel, God handles us the same way.

The shortest route to success is not always the best route because if we encounter issues along the way that we were not prepared or trained for, we will fail. God knows this. When I finally surrendered to God, I had to learn to trust God. I had to learn how to do without needed resources, work through seemingly impossible problems, endure working with challenging personalities on my job, and love those who willfully mistreated me. I had to develop that thick skin and persistence in prayer. Even though I had no tangible evidence other than God's word that everything was going to work out for me and my family's good. I heard a preacher say we need to develop "Even If" attitudes. Meaning, even if God does not deliver me from this, I will not bow to the world, throw in the towel or buckle under the pressure of life. I chose to face

---

[11] See Exodus 6:26, 7:4, 12:41, and 12:51

everything under the power and might of God and be that conqueror. Why? Because there are hurting people who need what God has put in me, and they need to see someone who is anchored to God and not drowning in the sea of life. I need to be that someone they ask, "How can you stay calm in the midst of this when everything around you is going crazy?" God's training, though at times it is tough, helped me to become a credible witness for his kingdom. I am boldly growing stronger and able to stand under the pressures of life. The bible tells us to endure hardship like a good soldier in Christ. If anyone ever plans on truly winning in life, we must first get connected to the source of life, which is God. Amassing great wealth, power, careers, and any other comfort in this world is not a real sign of living a winning life. Sure working hard and being a responsible person is right. Still, if your accomplishments are void of God's hand, they are all useless. The bible says:

> *Unless the Lord builds a house, its builders labor over it in vain; unless the Lord watches over a city, the watchman stays alert in vain. Psalms 127:1 (HCSB)*

I have often heard the term "Self-Made Man." Well, I would like to introduce another saying, "God Made Man." When I depended on myself, I messed up everything. I needed God's help. God has blessed me beyond what any dollar amount, human achievement, and prestigious accolade could have ever done for me. I am not saying these things are bad, but it is not my testimony. If any of you who are reading this book have achieved this status, give thanks to God. Use that influence He has given you to advance His kingdom. I know some would probably say, I am using religion as a crutch to excuse what may appear to the world as a lack of success. News flash, God has made me tremendously successful, and I am not using this as some religious cliché. Am I a millionaire? No. Do I own or manage a successful business? No. Am I a rising socialite? No. However, I have the God of the universe who owns it all, whose resources are limitless and cannot be repossessed by any man. I have a beautiful full-figured, Godly wife who loves me. I have four beautiful children and three grandchildren. I am healthy, I am gainfully employed, and I am God's ambassador to a dying world.

PERSISTENCE

I must admit that I am not a fan of obstacles and resistance concerning navigating through life. All things being fair, I personally would like for all of my life affairs to come together problem-free. However, I have come to learn that this is not realistic, and as we walk with God, He will allow and orchestrate obstacles to develop us. Like I have said, God is the ultimate life coach with an impeccable track record for developing His people. God wants His people to be persistent in doing His will. Persistence is the obstinate refusal to quit, no matter what problems or obstacles one encounters. We live in a time where people are quitting on just about anything that opposes their point of view. I do not have to quote stats in regards to marriages and other commitments; all we have to do is look and listen to what is going on around us. In the past, I use to look upon someone else's achievement and say things like," They are so lucky, everything seems to go their way." My thinking was ignorant because I did not consider the amount of commitment, sacrifice, and persistence they probably had invested in accomplishing their goal. Like many, I wanted a reward without sacrifice. I went through most of my adult life, thinking that things were just supposed to happen for me. Therefore, I experienced a lot of frustration when life did not yield me my American dream. I would start projects, but as soon as the fire would be turned up on my circumstances, I would quit. I was like a pinball bouncing around between obstacles instead of plowing them down as I faced them. I lacked persistence, and God was so gracious to help me to obtain it.

When I openly accepted God's assistance in building persistence, developing patience was a given. Patience and persistence go hand in hand; you cannot have one without the other. Patience says I will remain calm while facing my obstacle, and persistence says I will not let this issue stop me. I will continue to move forward. In other words, I am expected to walk calmly while moving forward in the face of obstacles. Too often, challenges in life are looked upon as being a negative thing, and as long as we keep this point of view, we will never walk in the purpose that God has for us. My Pastor would often say that we can never rise above our level of thinking. This principle holds true for both the Christian and non-believer alike. I had to see my problems as they were. They are training sessions that will help me to build a more robust persistence level. They are designed to help us move forward in the face of life's challenges and to trust God no matter what. I have experienced some setbacks during this process and even while writing this book. Let's get something straight, we will have times of lack. Jesus even said that at times, we will have trouble (See John.16:33). Jesus also tells us not to get down about it, but to cheer up because He has overcome every challenge we have and will face in life. God knows that we do not like experiencing difficulty. That is why we need to ensure that our suffering is not self-induced; though all too often, most of the challenges we face are. The funny thing is that some of our hardships happen because we try to take short cuts to avoid difficulties and problems. For example, as we age, we may put on extra weight for many reasons. It may be tempting to alleviate this problem by going on fad diets, taking some miracle pill, or getting an operation. These things may appear to work initially, but they never really fix the real issue and can cause more harm than benefit. Instead of seeking a quick fix, it would be far better to find quality solutions to get the weight off and a plan to keep it off. This process may be time-consuming and involve doing things that bring temporary discomfort. Still, the end result is much better with fewer complications. This is true of anything we face in life. We will experience challenges and setbacks as we pursue our God-given purpose. It is how we respond to these challenges that make us or break us. When I worked offshore, I was told by one of my supervisors that I was going to get run off the rig if my performance did not improve. I was a hard worker. I was not lazy, and I could perform every function as it pertained to my job except for piloting the ROV (remotely operated vehicle) with proficiency. I worked at it and tried my best, but for some reason, this was a great challenge for me. If any of you have ever worked offshore, you know that some of the personalities out there can be very blunt. They are unapologetic about what comes out of their mouths. I had days when I went back to my room and cried because it took everything within me, not have an outburst of anger. Instead of becoming bitter and hateful, I sought God more. I started thanking Him for being my God and my Father. I started praying for those who willfully took every chance to magnify my weaknesses. Instead of shrinking back, I pressed in and was determined to become better. I wanted to be better not for my coworkers, but because I knew God had given me a brilliant mind, and I could do all things through Him. In the end, I did get better at piloting the ROV (remotely operated vehicle). However, I did not make the cut and was crewed down from that assignment. I was not laid off, but I did not have a permanent assignment anymore and bounced around from one small project to another. On the surface, this looked like a defeat, but with every project they had put me on, I attacked with God-given persistence and diligence. Although this was not my preferred outcome, I learned that when we face obstacles from God's perspective and with perseverance, He opens doors to better opportunities for us. I ended up leaving that employer on my own terms and obtained employment locally, whereby I can be home with my family daily. God is good!

THANKFULNESS AND PRAISE

If there is one thing I have come to learn about God, is that He loves a heart of obedience, thanksgiving, and praise towards Him. I used to associate the phrase of saying the words "Thank You, Lord," with having a thankful heart towards God. Sadly, I found this not to be the case. There is a big difference in saying the right words and believing what you have said then acting upon it. I think that a lot of the religious jargon that we Christians use and speak is just something we regurgitate like a parrot because we heard it said in the church. So we started using it. At least, this is what I have discovered in my own life. When things are good, it is easy to be thankful and feel like you are blessed. Likewise, when things are bad, there is a tendency to feel condemned, and like God is far away. The problem with approaching life in this way is that it places us on an emotional roller coaster. Trust me, I have been in this place. One minute I am praising God, then the next I am saying woe is me. In this state of mind, it is impossible to please God and tap into the wonderful plan He has for our lives (See Hebrews 11:6).

What I said may not jive with today's train of thought, but as the bible says, God rewards those who diligently seek Him. Even some

Christians will argue, "Doesn't God pursue and seek us first?" The answer is yes, He does. Picture this, God is like a quarterback, and we are the receivers. Now God has all of the time in the world to give us the ball, He just wants us to run the route He has predetermined for us to catch the ball. There are defenders in between God and us. They are continually trying to keep us off our course from catching the ball. God is constantly saying, "Never mind them just run the route, you're going to catch the ball." Still, we tend to get distracted by these defenders (problems, obstacles, etc.) and decide to run a route that appears to put us in a better position to catch the ball. We end up on the other side of the field, and we never score. The question is, how do we get to a point whereby we learn to stay on the route God has for us despite our day to day issues? The answer is developing a heart of obedience, thanksgiving, and praise. This means throwing all of your religious clichés, jargon, and bandwagons into the garbage, allowing you to be open to ridicule and backlash from a culture that says, "Me First."

When we are truly thankful, we should also be obedient to God's will as well. I had the misconception that I had to like a thing or situation to be thankful. However, obedience is not about liking something, it is more about trust. Therefore, if I am genuinely grateful for everything God allows in my life, I will walk in obedience. Not because I like everything that happens to me, but because I trust God. When I believe God, I become thankful that He is in control of my life, and my future will be okay as long as I depend upon Him. In Jeremiah 29:11, God tells the prophet Jeremiah the good plans He has for Israel, and just like the children of Israel, God has great plans for us as well. Sometimes God's plans may allow us to experience discomfort or great success; either way, God expects us to be thankful and not bitter or prideful. There were times when I balled my fist up and shook it to heaven and said that infamous word "WHY?" God, being greater and higher than my thinking, did not yell at me or turn His back on me. He just simply allowed me to retake the test until I gave the proper response and action. If anyone has a right to say, "I told you so," it is God. However, God is not petty like us. He simply says, "Come, let us reason together." God understands our depravity and will not stoop to our level. We have to come up to His standard, and the only way to do this is to first accept

Jesus Christ as your Lord and Savior. Without accepting Christ, there can be no connection because the human form of reasoning will always be hostile towards God and His redemptive plan (see Romans 8:7). Without this connection, we can never be thankful, let alone obedient to God; the nature of man and our culture directly opposes the will of God.

As I said earlier, King David is often referred to as a "man after God's own heart." He knew the importance of having a thankful heart full of praise and adoration towards God. However, King David was not a perfect man. If you were to make a comparison between David and the previous King, King Saul. On the surface, you would say that the sins David committed before God was much worse than King Saul's. In our humanity, our way of defining what is good or bad is entirely different from God. If one were to look closer at why God rejected Saul, then you will understand why David was called a man after God's own heart. King Saul's ultimate trespass was pride and low self-esteem. He was easily influenced by the opinions of others. He was preoccupied with his image before the nation of Israel instead of God's. This fatal character flaw caused him to have disrespect for God's ordinances, which led to His disobedient behavior. In the book of Samuel chapter 15, God sends the prophet Samuel to confront Saul in regards to his disobedience and to disbar him as king over Israel. When Samuel starts questioning King Saul, he immediately starts giving excuses and does not own up to his wrong. Instead of admitting to what he has done upfront, he begins to pass the blame onto his men. Then when Samuel delivers God's sentence to Saul, it appeared that Saul was more concerned about his image before the elders and his people. He begged Samuel to pretend everything is okay so that the people wouldn't lose confidence in him.

David's heart was totally different from Saul's. Nathan, the Prophet, confronted David about his attempt to cover up his adulterous affair with Bathsheba and the murder of her husband. David made no excuses for what he had done and willfully accepted the punishment for his sins (see 2nd Samuel 12). Unlike Saul, the bible says that after receiving his sentence and after the death of the child born out of adultery, David cleaned himself up, went into the house of God, and worshipped (2nd Samuel 12:20). David and Saul committed great sins against God. Still, the main difference is that David had the heart to worship and honor

God no matter what and submitted to God's discipline. Just like David, we must not make excuses for what we have done. We must have the heart to obey God even when being corrected. <u>We must always have a heart full of gratitude and thanksgiving.</u> Let's be real, sometimes it is hard to be thankful while going through a storm, whether the storm is self-induced or of no consequence of our own. We must remember that while we live in time, we will experience trouble and must believe that God is still in control.

As I said in a previous chapter, my offshore experience was not good; it was a very challenging time for me mentally. I had two choices to make; either shrink back, become depressed and head back into the wilderness or muster up some strength and push forward. I just did not want to get by. I wanted to overcome, even if it meant that my circumstances would not change. Positive confession or thinking was not going to cut it; I needed something supernatural. I needed God's intervention. It's one thing to read God's Word from a positive point of view than from God's point of view. What I mean is I had to stop quoting God's Word as a means of positive confessions, but see it as something living and truly divine. When I see God's Word as alive and holy, I no longer simply view it as a good saying; I believe it and obey it no matter what. When I started doing this, I started making a practice of writing down three things I was thankful for each day and writing down something good about my day. I wrote prayer decrees for my children, grandchildren, and the young people in my church. I started praying for my coworkers and their well-being. I also started asking God to make me useful for His work. I took the attention off of my so-called problems and started praying and petitioning for other people, even those who did not care much for me. My goal was not to obtain a particular thing. I wanted to learn to be a truly thankful person, have a heart full of praise towards God, and obedient to His will even when it did not seem to be favorable for me. What I discovered was that God was allowing me to rise above my circumstances, and my family and I started experiencing abundant favor. Now get this, my day-to-day issues were still there, but God had begun opening doors that in no way I could explain or quantify.

Think of it like this, when a person starts to work out with weights, they may not be able to lift much in the beginning. Let's say that in the beginning, they can only lift 25 lbs, but after six months, they can lift 100 lbs. Now the 25 pounds they started with are still the same weight; that does not change. What changed was that person's ability to handle more resistance. So it is when we allow God to develop in us a thankful heart that is obedient to His Word and full of praise. Suddenly, we will find ourselves able to stand in what would typically cause a person to go insane. The psalmist says:

> *I would have lost heart, unless I had believed that I would see the goodness of the Lord In the land of the living. Wait on the Lord; Be of good courage, And He shall strengthen your heart; Wait, I say, on the Lord!*
> *Psalm 27:13-14 (NKJV)*

In conclusion, I can't lose heart or become discouraged when life appears to throw me a curveball or when I outright make a boneheaded decision. As I have stated before, yes, there are consequences for every decision we make, whether good or bad, but know this, God is greater than those consequences. Yes, we may have to experience some pain, but that does not mean that God is done with us. What we must make up in our minds is to learn from our mistakes and not grow bitter, depressed, or complain. We must allow God to complete His work in us. We do have a part to play in our training; we must participate and cooperate with God. God will not force or make us do anything, but He will stir the pot that will cause us to make a decision. Either we will rise to the occasion, or we will back down and tap out. Believe me, tapping out is not a good option because you will not move forward if you quit or stay in the past. Remember, Israel's 40-year wilderness experience and Lot's wife. I was not able to move forward until I started cooperating with God, stopped complaining, and let go of the past. I still have not arrived and faced a lot of challenges today, but I have made up my mind to move forward with God. So, I allow Him to work on my character, develop in me a toughness and persistence, and maintain a heart of thanksgiving. Still, each day He continues to work on me in all of these areas, and I am so thankful for it. Is it easy? Some days, but on others, it is not. So as we come to the close of this book. It has been my intention to share with you my life and how I am choosing to win each day. I've done my best to not make this another "how-to" book. But preferably present to you someone who is in between points A and B. Point A and B, is where we tend to quit if we allow the issues in our life's journey to block our path to God's purpose for our lives. As I said, it does not matter if you come from a prestigious family, have a college degree, or don't have a college degree, LIFE HAPPENS! To indeed win in life, we must believe and trust that God has a plan and purpose for our life. He will complete it in us if we do not quit.

> *I am sure of this, that He who started a good work in you will carry it on to completion until the day of Christ Jesus. Philippians 1:6 (HCSB)*

Be encouraged! You're going to win!

THE END

Printed in the United States
By Bookmasters